Caring for someone at a distance

Carers Handbook Series

Caring for someone at a distance

Julie Spencer-Cingöz

BOOKS

© 1998 Julie Spencer-Cingöz
Published by Age Concern England
1268 London Road
London SW16 4ER

Editor Gillian Clarke
Production Vinnette Marshall
Design and Typesetting GreenGate Publishing Services
Printed in Great Britain by Bell & Bain Ltd, Glasgow

First published 1998
A catalogue record for this book is available from the British Library.
ISBN 0–86242–228–0

Bulk orders

Age Concern England is pleased to offer customised editions of all its titles to
UK companies, institutions or other organisations wishing to make a bulk
purchase. For further information, please contact the Publishing Department at
the address on this page. Tel: 0181-679 8000. Fax: 0181-679 6069. E-mail:
addisom@ace.org.uk

Contents

About the author

Julie Spencer-Cingöz was brought up in Northumberland but now lives with her husband and daughter in Somerset, where she is the Human Resources Development Manager for a large care organisation. A registered nurse, she has much experience of working with older people, including managing a large residential home and community services.

Julie is frequently asked to speak at a variety of public forums nationwide on topics related to the care industry. She is co-author of a health and safety manual for care homes, and a regular contributor to publications aimed at people working in health and social care. In 1993 she was awarded a scholarship to study care management in the USA, and was the first winner in Somerset of a National Training Award.

Her personal experiences of caring for her own relatives at a distance, and her professional dealings with relatives of older people, prompted her to write this book.

Acknowledgements

I would like to thank the following: Caroline Hartnell for her advice about the structure of the book; Gillian Clarke, my editor, for her support and advice; Richard Holloway and Vinnette Marshall at Age Concern for their patience and help; Michael Addison at Age Concern whose suggestion it was that I write for them; and all those at Age Concern who read the manuscript and contributed helpful suggestions; Brian Samuels, Mrs A I Samuels, Anne Chiswell, Gill Ross, Jo Piper and Audrey Derrick who made invaluable contributions; Gillian Slaughter for her help with research; and Somerset Care for the opportunities to work with older people.

I would also like to thank the relatives for whom I have helped care over the years and whose experiences formed the basis of this book, and the many who shared their innermost feelings about caring at a distance. Thanks also to my husband and daughter for their support – and tolerance!

Introduction

There is now a wealth of much-needed information for carers living with their dependants. However, there is little on that increasingly common situation of trying to care for someone at a distance – which could be as far away as another country or as close as an annexe to your house.

A carer may be a relative, neighbour or friend, so the person to whom you have this long-term commitment may not always be an older relative. However, for simplicity, the term 'your relative' is used throughout the book.

The policies behind the NHS and Community Care Act 1990 encourage older people to stay in their own homes, but this is not to say that most of them have to struggle on alone. Only about 3 per cent of older people at home are estimated to have no contact at all with family or neighbours.

Many older people depend on others to help with basic tasks such as shopping. This means that there is a huge number of people – be they families or friends – who are taking on the role of caring at a distance in some form or other.

Families are becoming increasingly mobile. Work opportunities often require relocation; and children more often 'flee the nest' as society's expectations of the extended family role diminish. This mobility is not limited to children and grandchildren: indeed, the older person may relocate, to the area in which they spent their youth, or even the sunny shores of another country. Also, with modern times comes a relatively new phenomenon: divorce, remarriage, subsequent failure of the second relationship, and so on, so that a more diverse spread of relatives, step-relatives or ex-relatives may be involved in the role of distant carer.

Financial and work commitments may mean that you cannot visit your relative very often. When you get there, how do you find out what help is available in the area? How involved can you be in supporting your relative? How do you cope with the sense of frustration and guilt you may feel? What knowledge have you already about support structures available? This book examines the particular difficulties that can be encountered, and offers some practical advice and help.

Different help may be required at different stages of the care situation, and inevitably there is no one ideal solution. The advice given will not apply in all cases; for example, some parts of the book are written with an active older person in mind, whilst others are relevant to the care of someone with, say, dementia. The book also focuses on 'primary care givers', that is to say the carers who will be taking most of the decisions or providing most of the practical support. However, it will also be useful to those caring at a distance who may be termed 'secondary carers': those who can offer invaluable help and support to a more primary carer. Caring at a distance may range from an adult child living hundreds of miles away to a young student away from home temporarily during term time.

Caring at a distance brings with it unique problems and stresses. Commuting may be a strain; there may be a drain on your finances; you may feel particularly guilty at not choosing – or not being able – to be nearer to hand. You may already have heavy family commitments nearer to home, such as young children, or already caring for another older relative, or an ill or disabled person in the household.

If you have encountered a crisis, this book should prove a useful resource for ideas and advice. However, even if your older relative is still active and independent, reading this book should help you make contingency plans. If the situation breaks down, you will be able to alleviate much of the resultant stress and feel more capable – in fact, it is probably better to be reading this before rather than during a crisis.

Caring at a distance can result in a positive relationship for you and your relative. You may be able to agree more clearly what is and is not possible in terms of support than if you shared accommodation. And finding ways and means of enabling someone to retain their own home and a level of independence is one of the most supportive actions you may take. Moreover, not all older people believe that it is an adult child's duty to look after them; rather, adult children should lead their own lives, just as they may wish to.

1 Decisions to be made

Most people are aware that taking on a caring role will affect their lives, but often the full impact is not realised until they are embroiled in the situation and perhaps not able to see 'the wood for the trees'.

This chapter examines what caring at a distance may involve and the range of initial choices there may be. It looks at the pros and cons of these choices, and then discusses in more depth the practicalities of choosing to care at a distance.

Suggestions are made for establishing action plans and therefore a support network at the outset – both vital steps if you are to minimise future problems and stress.

Doreen

'I thought it would be relatively easy to care for her from a distance.'

'After all, she was fit and healthy and wouldn't have welcomed my interference, as she saw it. She'd always said I had my own life to lead. But it all changed after she had been in hospital. I wish I'd planned earlier for that kind of eventuality. I realised she was becoming more and more confused, and physically frailer, and I felt helpless at the other end of the phone. I decided I had to visit more frequently, but these visits became confrontational: we couldn't agree on the best courses of action. Worse

1

still, my husband and children felt neglected. If the children came with me at weekends they were bored and got sick of hearing the arguments. If they stayed at home, everyone resented the fact I wasn't sharing any of the good times: watching them win their football matches, going out together to the beach. I left them lists of things to do in the house to help me and we would have rows when I got home to find they weren't done.

'The visits every weekend began to put a strain on our finances: two cars were necessary, and petrol isn't cheap. I became more and more anxious, feeling inadequate and unable to help anyone, and I felt guilty at the resentment I started to harbour towards her. Why wouldn't she help me to help her, and move to be nearer my own home town?'

What might caring involve?

When first faced with having to support your older relative at a distance, you need to analyse the situation both as it is now and as you envisage that it might be in the future. If your relative is fairly active and mentally alert, they may have limited needs of you practically and/or emotionally, and the greatest problem could be that it can be a difficult experience for both of you to acknowledge that the situation could deteriorate at some point. Alternatively, you could be facing a painful reality now: that your relative is physically and/or mentally dependent on outside help, and that one or both of you need to greatly alter your lifestyle to accommodate the caring situation.

It may also be that what one of you believes is the easiest or best option is not shared or welcomed by the other.

Facing the options

When faced with the particular problems of caring at a distance it may seem that the best solution is to get rid of that distance, by one or the other party moving house. The main options are for you to move into their home or to a property nearer them or for them to move into your home or into what is popularly known as a 'granny annexe' to your own property or to accommodation nearer you.

It may be that your relative needs – or wants – the security of being cared for on a daily basis. This could mean that you have to help them choose sheltered accommodation or a residential or nursing home, either in their own locality or near yours.

Or it could be that the situation will remain as one whereby you will always live at a distance from them.

Susan

'I took early retirement but it was still not a reason to bring Mum to live with us. I don't want to be a carer day in and day out: I know I could never cope with that role. Selfish? Maybe. But I know I am being realistic. So whatever happens in the future, my choices will always revolve around my living a short distance away.'

Whatever choices you make, it is vital to be honest with yourself about your personality, your abilities as a carer, your relationship with your relative, your financial and work situation, and what you actually want to do. Equally important is to take account of your relative's wishes. A solution that is 'best' for you may not be so for them.

Moving in with you

This may be a decision you take at the outset, or it may be something you need to consider as the situation changes. It can be an ideal solution for all concerned. However, before your relative takes such a major step – which may mean that they lose existing local friends and networks and so become lonely – it is best to try to set up a long trial period. 'Ground rules' should also be established at the outset, such as how to share the cooking, access to communal areas so that everyone can have time on their own, and whether you can accommodate other visitors.

3

Anne

'I decided there was no other option. We have our rows of course – what family doesn't? And we've all had to make adjustments and compromises. Dad has always been there for me, so I have to be there for him.'

The benefits to your relative may include a sense of security, the reassurance that someone is there to keep an eye on their health, relief from financial strains and maintaining contact with younger generations. You may even find that there are benefits for you if your relative is fairly active, such as a helping hand in the house, cooking or even baby-sitting.

The financial situation of you and your relative may be such that you can have an annexe built on your property. This can provide an ideal compromise between increased reassurance and maintaining independence for all parties.

However, there may be a 'down' side, as the following daughter says.

Gillian

'Moving in with us seemed the most obvious solution at the time, but we have all paid the price. Dad has discovered that such 'sins' as rave music and teenage boyfriends exist, and is always trying to tell me how to bring up my daughter. She doesn't feel able to bring her friends home any more. My partner has left because of him, and I don't blame him. Nor do I blame Dad. I blame me – I wish I had found the courage to tell him he couldn't come to live with us.'

Other aspects to consider regarding your relative coming to live with you include:

■ How will you split the bills?
■ Are there 'rules' about shared spaces?

■ How will you help your relative to feel that this is their home now rather than being a guest who visits?

■ How can your relative develop a new social life while maintaining old links and friendships?

Although caring at a distance may not seem like an ideal solution to problems, it may still prove to be the most appropriate course of action once you have considered the position of everyone who might be affected by bringing your relative to live with you. On the other hand, the distance factor may prove too daunting or impractical. The key factor is not to commit yourself and your family to something you have not thought through.

For more *i*nformation

ℹ Carers Handbook Series: *Choices for the carer of an elderly relative* published by Age Concern Books.

You could move nearer

It may be that you consider moving house yourself to be closer to your relative. All the normal considerations related to moving home will apply, such as the impact on your or your partner's job, your family, and losing your own circle of friends. It is also worth remembering that there is no way to predict how long the caring situation will continue, and you could uproot everything for what may transpire to be a short period of time.

Moving into sheltered housing

It may be that your relative needs the 'halfway' option of independence coupled with the reassurance of someone keeping an eye on them, and in this instance sheltered housing schemes could be the answer. These either provide an alarm system connected to a central emergency contact point or have a warden who calls once a day to check that all is well, or both of these services are provided. Sheltered housing schemes may be rented or bought, and range from small flats or bungalows run by the local authority to luxury complexes operated by private companies and often advertised in up-market magazines.

For more *i*nformation

❶ Contact the local council housing department (in Northern Ireland, the Housing Executive).

❶ Age Concern England Factsheet 2 *Retirement housing for sale.*

❶ Age Concern England Factsheet 8 *Moving into rented housing.*

❶ *A Buyer's Guide to Retirement Housing* published by Age Concern Books.

Care homes

Although the NHS and Community Care Act 1990 has resulted in more emphasis being placed on special services providing help to support a person remaining in their own home, you or your relative may decide that the best course of action is for them to enter a care establishment. This can prove extremely reassuring for the carer at a distance, knowing that 24-hour professional supervision is available, although a 'down' side may be that carers may worry when they can't visit often.

Choosing a care home at a distance can be difficult, but in fact the same basic procedures should be followed whether you are looking for a home in your vicinity or that of your relative.

First, ascertain whether it is nursing or residential care that is required. These are often misunderstood, but basically a nursing home must have a trained nurse on duty 24 hours a day; if your relative is mentally or physically very frail or severely incontinent, this may be the best option. A residential home does not need a qualified nurse, but the manager must meet specifications laid down by the local authority as to their suitability to run a home, and the staff offer personal care such as bathing and assistance with toileting. Be guided by professionals such as social workers and district nurses as to the suitability of homes.

It is best to obtain a list of all the possible homes in the area; this is available free from the local health authority in the case of nursing homes, and from the local social services department for residential homes. (There are also various publications you can buy that publish lists, such as *The Care Homes Directory* (published on a local county basis) and *A–Z Care Homes Guide*).

The list should supply details such as whether or not there are staff on duty at night (waking night staff); the number of beds; and the category of registration – residential or nursing or 'dual' (ie registered with both social services and the health authority to provide residential and nursing care). Before you start to look, though, you should make out a checklist of your relative's needs. For example:

- Do they need residential or nursing care?
- Is it important that the home is near friends, other relatives, their church, etc?
- Is it more important to them to be nearer you?
- Would they prefer a large home with numerous amenities or a smaller, quieter home?
- How much can they afford to pay for their care?

For more *i*nformation

i Contact social services.

i Contact the Relatives Association (address on p 124).

If you plan to visit the area to inspect the homes, you will avoid wasting time by either you or your relative ringing up or writing first with a list of questions. Their answers will help you to draw up a short-list. If you ring, take note of the way the telephone is answered and how amenable they are to the idea of your visit. Some homes will invite you to call at any time, others will prefer you to make an appointment. This may be to ensure that they have time to spend with you to answer your questions, or it may be so that you do not have the opportunity to see the home 'warts and all'.

Preliminary questions may include:

- How much are the fees?
- Are they fully inclusive?
- Does the home work to recognised quality standards?

- How long is your waiting list?
- Is there a written resident contract?
- Can I talk to any of your current residents, or other relatives of people in the home?
- Can I still help with some caring tasks when I visit?
- Will my relative have a single room?
- Can residents lock their door?
- Can they decorate their room?
- Can they come and go as they please?
- What are the policies on pets; smoking; and visitors?

If your relative is to be admitted to a home some distance away from you, and you will therefore be unable to visit regularly, there are some additional factors that would be useful to explore:

- How will the home keep you in touch with what is happening? (For example, a regular phone call from a member of staff, or a newsletter?)
- Given that you may have had to travel a long distance to visit, will they welcome you to eat with your relative at the home?
- Will your relative have facilities to be able to make you a cup of tea easily?
- Do they have any accommodation for visiting relatives?
- Will you and your relative be able to go out together for visits?
- If your relative comes to stay with you for a holiday, are the full fees still payable?
- Is there a residents' phone?
- Could a phone be installed in your relative's room?
- Is the home dual registered (residential and nursing)?

If you have had to choose a residential home from a distance, you may not want to have to repeat the exercise if your relative's condition warrants a move to nursing care. So dual registration may be a deciding factor.

Always ask for an information pack to be sent to you. It's also a good idea to ask the health authority and social services if they publish their inspection reports on the homes. If they do, ask to see copies.

For more *i*nformation

i Age Concern England Factsheet 10 *Local authority charging procedures for residential and nursing home care.*

i Age Concern England Factsheet 29 *Finding residential and nursing home accommodation.*

i Counsel and Care Factsheet 5 *What to look for in a private or voluntary registered home.*

i Carers Handbook Series: *Finding and paying for residential and nursing home care* published by Age Concern Books.

Moving near you: into a home

Your relative may choose to reside in a care home in their own locality so that they can retain established links and friendships. On the other hand, moving them to a home closer to you may be preferable for you, giving the peace of mind that they are in a safe environment and making it easier for you to visit. However, it is wise to consider this step very carefully: entering communal living can be a traumatic experience even in the best of homes, and there may be added trauma if it is accompanied by a change of geographical area.

Alibeth

'She couldn't cope with the real cultural issues of living at the other end of the country.'

'It seemed a good idea at the time. We knew the home just down the road from us had an excellent reputation and it seemed ideal. Mum was in full agreement: she didn't want to be a burden and live with us; she knew the travelling was exhausting for us to visit; and she wanted to see the grandchildren more often.

'The home staff were brilliant, but even after a year she has not settled in. She misses her old friends more than she imagined she would, and it may

9

seem strange but there are definite differences in the pace of life, the dialects – you could say the culture – between the two ends of the country. For example, it may sound trivial but up here they refer to lunch as dinner. Where Mum lived, dinner is in the evening. She also has real difficulty in understanding some of the staff and residents. This kind of thing doesn't help her confusion.'

A further word of caution: if you are considering moving your relative into a care home in your own locality, there may be an issue concerning funding. If there is any possibility that the payment of fees will need to be supplemented by the local authority, you must discuss this fully with a social worker in your relative's area before choosing a home. Changes in legislation can affect the principles regarding financial support, and currently the 'sending authority' must agree to pay the price of care in the other area. Unless the authority agree that an assessed need is to be near relatives, they will be under no obligation to fund care in a more expensive area. Moreover, they may not be obliged to arrange or fund care if your relative has more than £16,000 capital and you can act on their behalf. In these circumstances the range of choice is limited unless your relative can pay for themselves.

Moving near you: into their own home

If your relative decides to move to a property in your vicinity, the same disadvantages in terms of leaving established links and friends may apply. However, the advantages will be ease of visiting for you and retention of independence for your relative. If this is the preferred course of action, you will need to consider how you will encourage your relative in creating new friendships and give support in maintaining old friendships. This latter may influence the choice of property; for example a two-bedroomed rather than a one-bedroomed home. Other aspects for your relative to consider will be the type of property to look for: new, easily maintained premises? Ground floor? Near facilities such as shops or a bus route? Help the Aged Retirement Property Service (HARPS) will provide free advice to buyers and sellers of retirement property nationwide.

Selling one home and buying another involves several costs, including:

- estate agents;
- solicitors;
- stamp duty;

- surveyors' fees;
- removal firm.

To find out which companies to use, if your relative has no suggestions, ask the neighbours for personal recommendations. Try ringing Talking Pages for a selection of numbers, or ask your own local firms if they are part of a national chain and can therefore deal with both the buying and selling aspects.

The practicalities of moving house

If you have to help your relative move from their house or flat, it is worth telephoning several removal firms to ask their fees. Ask for quotes, not estimates, and remember that there may be a premium rate for removals at a weekend. You and your relative need to agree beforehand how much of the arrangements they will carry out and how much you will do.

Moving from a council property

If your relative is moving from a council house to which they have made improvements, find out if there is a scheme whereby the council provides a partial rebate of their improvement costs.

Continuing to care at a distance

Having considered all the options, it may be decided that your relative will stay in their own home, perhaps with additional help.

Possible disadvantages include family support being too far away, loneliness, having to make expensive alterations to the home, or an increased risk to their health or safety. However, the advantages to your relative include staying among friends and a familiar environment as well as retaining independence, and the reassurance that you accept that your relative has a personal right to take risks.

2 Formulating your plans

Planning carefully can help minimise many later stresses. When you are formulating your plans for caring for your relative at a distance, it is important to make an objective assessment of their needs. These needs can be practical, emotional or spiritual, and will have differing priorities for action. Your plans will also depend on your relative's physical and mental health at any given time, and on your relative's willingness or ability to see things your way. Another factor will be the history of your relationship with each other and with others.

This chapter outlines some strategies that you can adapt in assessing your relative's needs and formulating your plans. It also stresses how your own needs must be taken into account within your planning stages in particular.

Taner

'I found I had my plans for the visit and he had his.'

'I knew that, every time I visited, I would be asked to go to the local supermarket, the hardware store and the cemetery, whereas I would have my own plans as to what I should be doing on the visits. The monotony of the visits to these three places used to frustrate me, but I realised it was actually quite helpful to have a regular framework. And if anything it made it easier to timetable in a special trip out each time. What soon became apparent was that I had not sat down with Dad to find out what his real needs were – I was making assumptions – and in fact it was easier to meet his needs than I had anticipated, because in reality they were fewer than I thought.'

Ashleigh

'There is something important to do on every visit, so a quiet chat becomes impossible to fit in. I've become a "hit and run" visitor, which is not good for our relationship.'

Building the foundation for future care

Probably the most important step you can take is to plan your visits carefully, taking into account the needs of your relative as perceived by you and by them, and your own commitments. How many visits can you realistically make? What holidays can you take from your work? How often can you supplement your visits with phone calls and letters? What previous commitments do you have? Which can you shelve and which need to be fulfilled whatever the circumstances? Who else can help you at home or at your relative's home? What ground rules do you need to set down about what you already know you will or won't be able to do?

Only when you analyse these factors honestly and realistically can you start to plan effectively: both about the frequency of visits and about the practical steps you can take when you get there. It may even mean programming in time for what almost become luxuries, for example a 'sit down' chat. Many carers write themselves little reminder notes to take with them, but a more detailed plan is very worthwhile. After all, your visits may not be as frequent as you might like, so you and your relative will want to make the most of your time together. (See also Chapter 5, 'How to get the most out of your visits'.)

It may help if you try to put something into your visits that both of you will enjoy; for example, a walk by the sea, a short car trip, a special shopping trip, a walk together round the garden. Don't worry if your visits always include some element of routine.

Get your relative's agreement

Try to gain your relative's agreement to your action plan. Make this your first objective of your next visit – to sit down together and decide on current issues and the steps you can take. There will be particular times when a visit may be even more valued; for example, for those widowed, anniversaries of their wedding, or the birthday of the deceased partner. By involving them in identifying and prioritising problems and by discussing possible solutions you are demonstrating that you care and that you can help practically, but that your relative is still making their own decisions.

Whenever you think you have identified a problem, stop and ask yourself, 'Who is this a problem for? Is it really a problem for my relative, or just for me?' For example, the house may not be as clean as it used to be. This may indeed be an area of frustration and therefore a problem for your relative, requiring some action. On the other hand, your relative may genuinely not be bothered by this, and, as long as there is no health or safety hazard as a result, it would be wrong for you to focus on this as a priority problem. Or, due to increasing mental frailty, your relative may be verbally aggressive towards you when you visit. Distressing though this may be, is it really a problem for them – or, understandably, you?

Be realistic

The first stage in planning is to determine *how often* you can afford to visit, both in terms of money and in time. Be realistic. Under-promise and over-deliver! Allow extra time for your journey if you are going to say what time you will arrive. It is probably better to be early than to have your relative worrying that you're overdue. Also, it is worse to promise to visit every other weekend and not be able to keep to the schedule, disappointing yourself and your relative, than to set a more infrequent pattern of visits, and fit in extra visits as and when possible. Remember, though, that surprise visits may not always be well received: an older person with a routine may not be as flexible as you are, or they may have their own plans made and not welcome the intrusion.

The next step is to *identify the problems* correctly, the third is to *prioritise them*, and the fourth is to *agree the appropriate course of action*.

You may need to carry out some practical tasks in your relative's house. As part of the planning process, look at how much time you can realistically spend, and break any major tasks into reasonable 'chunks' – for example, aim to paint one side of a building at a visit rather than be frustrated at not finishing the whole thing. Also aim to find the quickest solutions, which may be more expensive in terms of cost but better in terms of time.

Dot

'I simply don't have the time to do as thorough a job as I'd like.'

'Mum often asks me to do household maintenance jobs, and of course I'm happy to oblige. Sometimes the jobs aren't really urgent but they are important to her. But she lives five hours' drive away and by the time I've finished work, driven there, worked in her house or garden, driven home, and returned to work the next day with no "down time", I'm exhausted. So I must admit that sometimes the jobs aren't finished off to my real satisfaction. I've also found that I tend to use products at Mum's house which I wouldn't buy for my own; for example, I buy long-lasting toilet freshener blocks for her loo which don't keep the pan as clean as I'd like it to be but keep it fresh until my next visit. And when I'm painting I don't have time for sanding, stripping and undercoating, so I look for one-coat paints and just paint over. But she's happy with what I'm doing, so the message is really to find compromises and to be practical – there just isn't enough time for perfection.'

Do not wait for problems to occur

When compiling your action plan you may feel that you are prying into someone else's business. However, much of the information gained at the outset should help ease stressful times later on, and in order to provide help you really do need to know as much as possible. Make sure that you have a comprehensive list of telephone numbers to hand. Then, if you are informed that your relative has been admitted to hospital, for example, you can cancel milk, papers and so on promptly and easily. Even if there are no immediate high priority problems, have provisional action plans ready. Do not wait until you are desperate for help.

A suggested outline plan

Your initial action plan may look something like this:

Problem	Priority A/B/C	Solution: what/where/how	When we will review
Help needed in dressing	A	Home help needed. Contact social services for a list of registered providers.	One week
Some bills not paid	A	Catch up with payments. Set up direct debits where possible.	One month
Hands over £50 notes, thinking they are £5	A	Try to arrange visits to coincide with receipt of money (eg pension) so that notes of large denomination can be exchanged for smaller ones.	Three months
Now unable to drive	B	Apply to local authority for taxi tokens; check out voluntary driver services.	Two months

Family not helping	B	Call a family meeting at relative's house for next month; talk to minister and social worker for support. Allocate clear responsibilities.	Three months
Broach subject of power of attorney	C	Make joint appointment at family solicitor's. Talk to family.	Three months
Ran out of oil. Needed emergency delivery	C	Arrange delivery at set intervals.	Six months
Not accessing concessions	C	Check out offers on next visit.	Three months
Where are all the documents?	C	Send for copies of certificates/find records; bank/NI/NHS/Will. Help to check and update on next visit.	One month

You may also need to formulate a 'seasonal' action plan. For example:

- Pre-autumn   Check flues/chimneys
- Pre-winter   Check salt/grit available; pipes lagged
  Visit to sort out writing and sending
  Christmas cards, Christmas shopping
  (including ordering from catalogues)
- Pre-spring   Check garden equipment

3 Minimising risks

One aspect of caring at a distance is often that a great deal of time is spent worrying about what might go wrong in your relative's household.

If a crisis occurs at your relative's home and you live some distance away, you may find it extremely difficult to deal with. Indeed, too many emergencies occurring may tip the balance from your relative maintaining their independence in their own home to needing to go into care.

Hopefully, the alarming situations shared by carers in this chapter will not happen to your relative. However, as prevention is always better than cure, you can use the information to prevent or minimise health or safety crises occurring.

This chapter looks at general safety measures in the home and ranges from preventing hypothermia and falls to deterring burglars.

The practical advice given should help your relative retain their independence by enabling them to remain safely in their own home. Always remember, however, that maintenance of your relative's independence may mean some balanced risk taking.

Keeping warm

The homes of older people may be too cold in the winter. The recommended minimum temperature is 21°C; it may be worth buying a room thermometer to help you check on your visits. If it is likely that your relative may forget to turn on the heating in winter, or may have difficulty in using heaters safely, a central heating system kept on permanently or controlled by a neighbour may be a solution.

If the heating fuel is oil or coal, arrange for regular deliveries rather than waiting for the fuel to run low before re-ordering.

If the house is very cold and expensive to heat, it may be wise for your relative to consider living in one room only, by moving the bed into the living room. Draught excluders can be expensive and are not always necessary: if your relative has little income, they could use such items as old coats to block draughts under doors (but be careful that the coats do not become obstacles that might be tripped over). Fit kitchen foil behind any central heating radiators to reflect heat back into the room. Also check that there is adequate loft insulation and lagging of pipes: grants for this may be available.

Note The dangers of hypothermia cannot be overemphasised: older people are particularly at risk because their body's controlling mechanisms do not work as well when they are cold.

For further *i*nformation

i Carers National Association information sheet 19 *Renovation grants.*

i Age Concern England Factsheet 13 *Older home owners: financial help with repairs and adaptations.*

Safety in the home

As people grow older they usually relax more in their own home than, say, out in the street or in a strange environment. However, they may move and react more slowly, not to mention the possibility of forgetfulness, so life at home may become fraught with danger. Your relative may still be trying to do things that are now more of a struggle or for which their home is not well equipped; for example, bending over to reach plugs.

Accidents in the home

Home accidents account for just over one-third, or 35 per cent, of all fatal accidents, and those at greatest risk are children under five and pensioners. Some 20 per cent of home accidents occur in the living or dining room, 17 per cent in the garden, 16 per cent in the kitchen, 12 per cent on stairs, 11 per cent in the bedroom and 24 per cent elsewhere, such as the bathroom.

These figures may seem alarming but remember that many older people live safely in their own homes. Nevertheless, balancing your relative's safety with their right to remain independent and take risks may well be a difficult issue to resolve. A definition of a hazard and risk may be helpful here:

■ a *hazard* is anything with the potential to cause harm, whilst
■ a *risk* is the likelihood that harm may be caused.

Many things in a home may be potential hazards, and some may constitute real risks to older people – but it has been said that if you take away all risks then you take away life.

How can you minimise the risks?

Many practical solutions involve buying gadgets aimed at protecting children. This is not a question of treating your relative like an infant, merely of using whatever is best. Try visiting your local Mothercare or Boots store – there you will find many useful and reasonably priced aids, including:

- cooker guards;
- safety glass/film;
- plug-in nightlights;
- fire guards;
- furniture corner covers;
- non-slip rug mesh.

As well as applying safety film to the glass in doors and partitions, use it for glass-topped tables, shower screens and greenhouse glass panes. Another idea to consider is a safety gate placed at the top of the stairs at night if your relative is confused and might fall down them: if you visit twice a day or if home help is provided every night and morning, this may be feasible.

Ensure that smoke detectors are fitted (choose one bearing the British Standard number BS5446, and remember not to fit one in the kitchen or bathroom, because the steam might activate the alarm). A carbon monoxide detector should be fitted if gas, oil, coal or calor gas is used.

Two other steps you can take are to check that air bricks and ventilators have not been obstructed, and turn down the hot water thermostat to 54°C (130°F) to prevent the danger of scalding.

Providing sufficient heating in the house is vital, but safety is equally important. People over the age of 60 represent the greatest proportion of deaths caused by clothing catching fire, almost half of these involving electric fires. As well as encouraging styles of clothing less likely to pose fire risks (eg discouraging wide sleeves and loose scarves being worn in the house), check that any heaters used conform to current British safety standards: for example, calor gas heaters to BS5258 parts 10 and 11; good quality paraffin to the standard BS2869 CI; and electric heaters that have a safety cut-out if they are tipped over.

Try to discourage your relative from buying second-hand gas and electrical goods: they may be cheaper but they may also be faulty.

For further *i*nformation

ℹ️ Contact the Royal Society for the Prevention of Accidents (RoSPA) for leaflets on accident prevention (address on p 124).

ℹ️ Contact your local health visitor for practical advice and leaflets.

ℹ️ Contact an occupational therapist for assessment and advice.

Mai-Ling

'He accused me of tempting fate.'

'Father is superstitious and was furious when he realised that I was going around the house checking all the hazards and suggesting steps we could take to prevent accidents. He said I was tempting fate, that nothing had ever happened before to him so there was no need to change anything now.

'I could see that his health was deteriorating, both physically and mentally, but he wouldn't admit that there was anything wrong. I was so worried that he might fall and be unable to get help, or that he'd do something like set the house on fire – he'd become so careless.

'One day he did fall. In fact, he fractured his hip. Luckily, by then I had managed to persuade him to have an alarm system installed. He was able to summon help immediately he fell, and he's now back home from hospital and recovering well. He would still never admit that the alarm is a godsend, and of course he took the opportunity to tell me I'd brought the accident on because of my actions! But I can live with that.'

Alarms

If there *are* any emergencies, it is reassuring to know that your relative can call for help quickly, and for that reason one of the most useful gadgets around is a community alarm. It can be used to summon help in a variety of situations, although possibly the commonest one, about which families worry the most, is that of their relative falling. Alarm systems vary: some have a pull cord in a suitable position in the rooms, some are activated by an alarm worn on the wrist or around the neck and are waterproof so can be worn in the bathroom. They are connected to the telephone system so that, when the alarm button is pressed, a call goes to the control centre. The person needing help does not have to struggle to the telephone. Age Concern have a system, Age Concern Aid-Call, and a factsheet about aids – Age Concern England Factsheet 42 *Disability equipment and how to get it*. Social services may supply alarms, or they can be purchased privately. Help the Aged can supply information on the availability of alarms, and may in fact be able to obtain one if there is no local scheme.

Insurance cover

It could be worth checking your relative's insurance cover now, before any falls occur. You may wish to look at policies such as the 'Injury Cash Plan' from Age Concern.

Lighting

Good lighting is essential, so it will pay you to fit the maximum wattage bulb each light fitting will take. To prevent light bulbs going out frequently and causing inconvenience to your relative, you may wish to invest in energy-efficient bulbs that, although costing more than standard bulbs, use less power and last longer (there are some on the market reputedly lasting ten years). If your relative tends to forget, or is reluctant, to switch on lights at dusk, lights with sensors that automatically switch on at dusk and off at dawn could be one solution; alternatively, fit a timer to table lamps.

Luminous tape around the light switches will make it easier to find them in the dark.

Bedside lamps can be extremely useful, making it unnecessary to get out of bed in the dark. You can now buy the type that is switched on and off simply by touching the lamp. A less expensive option is to have a torch by the bedside.

Electrical safety

While looking at electrical safety in the house, check that plugs are wired correctly and contain the appropriate fuse, with no bare wires between the plug and covered cable, and that flexes are not frayed. Check that power points are not overloaded, and that flexes do not run under carpets. Plugs with special grip handles may be a useful buy. Coiled flexes may be needed on appliances such as kettles, or you may consider a cordless iron and kettle to be a good investment. Whatever the type of kettle, make sure that it has a cut-out facility to prevent its being left to boil dry. Pay particular attention to any electric blankets in use, and check for frayed flexes. It may be useful to plug it into a socket with a residual current device (RCD). If the blanket is not currently in use, check that it has been stored away without creasing.

Other measures you might like to consider include having the power points in the house moved from the skirting board to a higher position (perhaps waist height, so avoiding the need to bend over), and buying an RCD for power tools, lawnmowers etc if they are still being used. You could attach a reminder label to the RCD about its use at the power point, or, better still but more expensive, buy RCD plugs and attach one to each specific appliance. These are available in electrical and DIY stores.

It is especially important to check on electrical safety at Christmas. Before the season begins, help your relative to check the decorations – that there is no broken glass – and in particular that the Christmas lights have no damaged wires and are not broken in any way. A three amp fuse should be in the plug, and an RCD and of course a smoke alarm give extra peace of mind.

Kitchen safety

For the kitchen, it may be worth buying carousels to store pans, vegetables and so on. A timer with a loud ring is also a useful item. The best can openers, which can be wall-mounted or electrically operated, leave no jagged or sharp edge on the tin; they are available from department and hardware stores. Because older people may be prone to blackouts if they tilt back their heads, it would be wise to discourage your relative from storing items on high-level shelves, and climbing on chairs or stools to reach items: one solution could be to store only decorative ornaments on top shelves, rather than items such as storage jars which may be needed.

A key safety factor to check in the kitchen is that fluids such as bleach and detergents have not been decanted into soft drinks bottles.

Some people who are unsteady on their feet feel more secure if they can sit down to prepare food. If a chair is too low, special stools are available: consult an occupational therapist.

If your relative is partial to deep-fried foods, one of the best things you can do is persuade them to use an electric deep-fat fryer. Remember to supply a fire extinguisher in the kitchen and perhaps a fire blanket too (look for British Standard number BS6575). Even if your relative is unable to learn how to use them, they could come in useful if a fire is caused and someone else tries to help.

Regular checks

You may need to help your relative budget for and book regular servicing of all appliances such as the cooker, fires, the central heating system and paraffin heaters – and electric blankets, if you have not been able to discourage their use. This is particularly important for your peace of mind when you are not around to keep a watchful eye on them. Do not forget things such as occasionally used calor gas heaters; they can be handy if there is a power cut but might be overlooked if they are not used regularly. These heaters can usually be taken to a shop for a check (see in Yellow Pages under 'Bottled Gas Suppliers') or can be checked by a registered gas installer (call CORGI, the Council of Registered Gas Installers, for more information). Remember also to book cleaning – at least annually – for chimneys and flues, and on your visits do a spot-check to ensure that pilot lights are not out. Incidentally, all gas supply companies can carry out a free safety check on gas appliances and installations if the person meets certain criteria (eg they are over 60 years old and live alone or with someone else who qualifies) and provided their name and address is entered on the company's special register. Telephone numbers are in the phone book under 'Gas'. Of course, the safety check is not a substitute for regular servicing.

Note Make sure that you know the location of the isolation switches for electricity and gas in your relative's house, as well as the main stopcock. It is also wise to leave a note of their location with a neighbour.

For more *i*nformation

i Contact the relevant utility companies for details of current schemes, including special registers

Other areas of the house

Another potentially hazardous area is the bathroom. Check that any handrails are securely fixed to the wall, replace any slippery vinyl flooring with carpeting, and buy a rubber bath mat or the decorative stick-on rubber grips.

On the staircase check that it is well lit and that carpets are not loose or frayed. You may wish to install a second handrail.

In the bedroom check that the bed is the right height for your relative: when sitting on the edge of the bed, the soles of their feet should be touching the floor. While checking this, do ensure that slippers are not old and loose.

Do not forget to check that paths outside the house are even and moss-free (a cheap way to wash down paths is to use a strong solution of washing soda and hot water). As winter approaches, make sure there is a bucket of sand or grit available in case of ice.

Shirley

'I became an expert at telling "white lies".'

'Every time I tried to do something to improve the safety of my elder sister she would find a reason why I couldn't. Of course she resented what she saw as my interference. After all, how many of us would welcome occasional visitors to our house rearranging our possessions? I became an expert at inventing reasons for doing things that did not imply any hint of looking at her safety. For example, when she refused to have non-slip stick-ons in the bath, I waited a while until the bath surface was rather scratched and she agreed to them as decorative measures. And she desperately needed to have a less cluttered living room but wouldn't allow me to move any furniture. So on her birthday I bought her a large floor-standing plant for the corner of the room, which gave me a legitimate excuse for moving everything around.'

You may see many steps that could be taken to improve the safety of your relative in their home environment, but you may have to negotiate, and to think laterally about their introduction!

For more *i*nformation

❶ Carers National Association information sheet 14 *Equipment to aid daily living*.

❶ Help the Aged information sheet 15 *Equipment for daily living*.

❶ The Alzheimer's Disease Society (address on p 119) can provide information on sources of safety equipment.

❶ Contact the Disabled Living Foundation (address on p 121) for a wide range of leaflets.

❶ Care and Repair (address on p 120) provide information on grants available for repair and home improvements.

Securing the home

You may think that crimes, especially violent crimes, are frequent and that they are becoming even more so. However, it must be stressed that crimes against older people are relatively uncommon.

Obviously the police are the best people to give you and your relative advice about their property, but steps you could take immediately include:

- a spy-hole in the door;
- a door chain on all outside doors;
- a mortise deadlock on the door;
- a mortise sashlock on side and back doors with extra bolts top and bottom;
- espagnolette or casement bolt on french windows;
- window locks;
- an automatic time switch for lights;
- padlock and hasp on the garden shed;
- an extra telephone in the bedroom;
- outdoor detector lights;
- gravel and/or thorny bushes below windows and next to perimeter fences;
- checking under doormats and flower pots to ensure that a key has not been left there;
- security marking of items such as the TV;
- photographing valuables;
- noting serial numbers of goods.

Sometimes there are schemes available via local councils or organisations such as Age Concern to help fund security measures. Also, don't forget to display labels on windows showing that the house has security measures: these are available from the police station or Neighbourhood Watch. When installing or changing locks, be sure to use only approved locksmiths (check with Yellow Pages or Talking Pages).

Doorstep security

If your relative lives in a flat with a labelled door entry system, ensure that the name plate gives no indication of a person living alone, and does not give a title such as 'Miss' or 'Mrs'. Sometimes it's possible to guess that an older person lives in the house or flat by their external condition – the front garden is not cared for, and fences or doors and windows needing painting.

A useful contact and source of advice is the local crime prevention officer, who may well visit in plain clothes. Some older people respond more positively to advice if it is given by a police officer in uniform; if this is the case, you could ask if the local community police officer could call in instead, or to reinforce any advice given.

Len

'We'd told her time and time again not to let strangers in the house, and so did the crime prevention officer.'

'She didn't think of the crime prevention officer as a real policeman because he didn't wear a uniform, and she paid the price. She let a "nice young man" in, and he stole from her purse and assaulted her. It took this, and a local uniformed policeman, to get the message of home security across to her.'

Also, make sure that the local Neighbourhood Watch scheme is aware of your relative's circumstances: the local co-ordinator will probably 'keep an eye out' for your relative. The scheme, which is organised with the help of the police, provides useful information on home security devices.

Dealing with contractors

If you can persuade the neighbours to keep an eye out for anything suspicious, this is invaluable. We sometimes hear stories of, say, builders who arrive unannounced and persuade the person to pay for emergency work that was never really required. To help prevent this, you could arrange with the neighbours that you will always inform them of any contractors/repair persons scheduled to work there.

If you need to contact reliable contractors on your relative's behalf, it can be daunting simply to choose one from a telephone directory. A more reassuring step may be to access a scheme such as that run by the AA, or certain insurance companies or credit cards such as

Barclaycard, whereby they maintain a list of reputable contractors in each area. Alternatively, the local Care and Repair scheme might be able to suggest local contractors.

If you do have to request any workpeople to visit, make sure you establish some 'ground rules' at the outset – possibly in writing. For example, they will contact you first before embarking on each stage of their work, or they will deal with the moving and replacing of any furniture that your relative may not be able to manage.

Utility companies are geared to help

The utility companies nowadays are very much geared to helping older people with home security, for example by providing a password system. (They will wait at the door for longer than usual, if they know that an older person has mobility problems.) Contact the local branches of these companies for details.

Karen

'We couldn't agree on a password that she would remember. However, we eventually hit on her pet name for me, which she only ever uses between us in private. So now the gas man can tell her that "Floss" sent him.'

Burglar alarm systems

Lindsay

'He forgot he had a burglar alarm.'

'I had already installed an alarm, and gone to great lengths to show him how to use it, reinforcing this at every visit. It was a very simple one which only required a key to be turned to activate it. It was only after he was burgled one night that I found out he had forgotten he had an alarm – he said he had wondered what the box was on the wall. I learned a lesson – to make sure a large reminder label is attached to all pieces of equipment like this.'

There are numerous burglar alarms on the market. Those that are set by code numbers are not really suitable for an older person who has a degree of confusion, so the best options are probably the ones operated by the turn of a key. Make sure that the alarm system incorporates an outside box; its presence will help deter burglars.

If you fit a burglar alarm for your relative, make sure that it meets BS6707 standard if it is a DIY alarm or BS4737 if it is installed by a professional.

Personal alarms

A personal alarm system, such as are available from Age Concern or Help the Aged, can help ensure the security of your relative. They are useful to call for help if your relative feels ill or sustains an injury, but if there is an intruder in the house they can be activated and therefore act as a deterrent. Try to persuade your relative to consider such an alarm sooner rather than later as a reaction to an incident. It will help provide emotional security for both of you.

Security of money

Another area of concern may be the security of money. The obvious things are to remind your relative not to keep large sums of money at home, and on your visits it may be prudent to help make the bed and check typical hiding places such as under the mattress. If you are worried about your relative becoming forgetful, and spending large amounts of money or not waiting for their change in the shops, why not make a point of getting to know their local shopkeepers on one of your visits and highlighting the problem? You could also ask the local post office to issue only notes of small denominations in their pension. It is also possible for your relative to authorise someone – yourself or a home help for example – to act as an agent to collect their pension.

For more *i*nformation

ⓘ Contact the Alzheimer's Disease Society for a range of useful leaflets (address on p 119).

ⓘ Age Concern England Factsheet 33 *Feeling safer at home and outside.*

ⓘ The local police station can provide information about crime prevention and Neighbourhood Watch.

Security marking

If possessions are stolen despite your security measures, it can help if you have marked them with your relative's postcode, using a pen that shows up under ultra-violet light. It may also help to take photos and write descriptions of any valuables: you could store these at your own home or at the bank. Remember to carry out these steps on any garden equipment stored in sheds.

Other measures

Although it may seem obvious, do check that you have a spare key for all doors, and that a trusted neighbour also has a set of keys. Check regularly that there is no key hidden in obvious places such as under plant pots or doormats. You may also wish to install a box over the letterbox inside to discourage thieves from putting their hands through and trying locks. (The added bonus of one of these boxes is that your relative does not need to bend down to pick up letters.)

Also check that your relative has house insurance – and keep details of the policy at your own home. One insurance company's research indicates that about 20 per cent of older people have no – or insufficient – contents insurance.

For further *i*nformation

ⓘ Contact Age Concern Insurance Services at Garrod House, Chaldon Road, Caterham, Surrey CR3 5YW, for details of their insurance policies.

Personal security

As well as security of the house, you may need to consider the security and safety of your relative if they become forgetful, or start wandering and get lost. This can be one of the most stressful things for a distant carer to cope with. Nevertheless, there are steps you can take in advance, so that if this does happen you are prepared.

Means of identification

Make sure that a printed card with your relative's address, and perhaps other helpful information (eg your contact number), is in their wallet or handbag. A more discreet way of doing this is to ensure that, if they carry a diary – which is a very useful tool anyway – their address is filled in at the front. There will probably also be a space for a contact number for you. This is an ideal, dignified way of providing reminders, which might include the name of the neighbour with the spare key (and a locksmith's number just in case), the name and telephone number of a taxi firm, the doctor's telephone number, and so on. You might also consider buying an identity bracelet or chain to be worn. Or, for a female, you could attach a key ring to the zipper of her handbag. The type that has the address inside it is probably best – most people would recognise it and look inside if they were trying to help your relative. (An added advantage is that it will make the handbag zipper easier for arthritic hands to open.)

A disadvantage to ensuring that this information is kept in a handbag or wallet is that, if it is stolen, the details will be made available to a burglar. It is another matter of weighing up the risks.

Photos

It is also wise to be prepared and to have to hand, or to leave with a neighbour, copies of a recent clear photo of your relative – just in case. The original photo can be colour photocopied as a cheaper option to reprints. If you ever receive a call to say that your relative is missing, you can arrange for the photos to be circulated to the police, accident and emergency departments, local taxi firms, and bus or train stations.

Ask others to help

Selina

'She kept losing the car, and local taxi drivers became a vital lifeline.'

'My mother started to regularly forget where she had parked the car, and would panic and call the police, who naturally got fed up. The solution – because she still refused to give up driving – was to encourage her to call the same taxi company. We ensured she had the number in her bag. The driver would pick her up, drive around to find her car (never very far away) and follow her home. We had an arrangement whereby I would pay for this monthly, using her bus tokens which in her area are accepted by taxi firms. To be fair, the firm were wonderful – I suppose it was regular work for them after all! Luckily, Mum eventually gave up driving on the advice of her doctor (prompted by me) – who told her that her insurance company would be unlikely to cover her in future, after her involvement in an accident.'

Within our society, being able to drive is a mark of maturity and responsibility. Having this right taken away can be a major blow. If you are worried about your relative's driving abilities, contact their GP for advice, or the DVLC (address on p 122).

For more *i*nformation

ⓘ Contact the Alzheimer's Disease Society for a range of useful leaflets (address on p 119).

ⓘ Age Concern England Factsheet 33 *Feeling safer at home and outside.*

4 What to look for when you visit

It is almost inevitable that much of your visiting time will involve checking various aspects of your relative's welfare. You will be looking for signs to reassure yourself that the situation is stable or has improved; if deterioration has occurred, you will want to take action as soon as possible.

Some of the checks you may carry out have been covered in the previous chapter, 'Minimising risks'; this chapter focuses on health aspects you may encounter. By recognising signs and symptoms of physical and mental illness and knowing what proactive steps you can take, you may be able to prevent some major health problems.

Also included in this chapter is information about helping your relative in maintaining a healthy diet, with numerous practical tips.

Pets can play an important role in the lives of people, and if your relative has a pet you may find that your caring at a distance includes looking out for its welfare. The chapter therefore goes on to give advice on what to look for so that you can support your relative in caring for their pets.

Dealing with incontinence

If you can visit only occasionally, you may well notice any changes in your relative's health more readily than if you visit more often. It is probably a good idea to give yourself a mental checklist of signs of any worsening in their physical state. One of the most obvious may be that you notice the tell-tale signs of incontinence. There may be a smell of urine in the house for the first time. This can be one of the most difficult personal health problems to discuss, despite the fact that, in Britain alone, an estimated three million adults have incontinence problems.

Bob

'The smell hit you as soon as you walked in.'

'At first there was just a stale smell on occasions. I wasn't really convinced that there was a serious urinary problem. As it wasn't too bad I didn't bother broaching the subject with him. Cowardice really – I just didn't have a clue where to start. I mean, you can't just walk up to someone and say, "You smell".

'He had always been so careful about his personal hygiene that when I tried to even suggest there may be a waterworks problem he hit the roof. He said I was insensitive – that I only visit three times a year so how dare I think I had a right to bring up the subject. He obviously knew in his heart of hearts that there really was a problem but his pride would not let him admit it.

'He put all the blame on the poor cat.'

Whether you feel you can discuss the problem openly depends on your relationship. If you feel you cannot, or that you are getting nowhere, contact the district nurse (or perhaps the GP) who may be able to find a reason for a routine check-up. In the meantime, try to take notice of as much as possible so that you can help their diagnosis and therefore treatment. For example:

- Does coughing or sneezing seem to cause leakage? (could be stress incontinence)
- Do they not reach the toilet in time? (could be urge incontinence)
- Is there dribbling and leakage? (could be overflow incontinence)
- Is there any bedwetting? (enuresis)
- Is there leaking from the bowel? (faecal incontinence)

It may turn out to be functional incontinence, whereby the urinary system is working perfectly but mobility problems prevent the person getting to the toilet in time. It will also help the nurse to know such things as how long there have been any problems and how often your relative seems to use the toilet.

Most cases of incontinence are curable or significantly improved; some are caused by simple short-term problems such as an infection. If your relative needs help to come to terms with incontinence, this is available from district nurses, continence advisers, occupational therapists, the Continence Foundation and the Disabled Living Foundation's Incontinence Advisory Service (addresses on pp 120 and 121). Following specialist advice, steps that can be taken may include using protective pads, using protective sheets for the bed, or providing a commode or even chemical toilet near to the bed. There is an increasing amount of support available in most areas to help tackle the problem.

For more *information*

i Contact the Continence Foundation (address on p 120).

i Age Concern Factsheet 23 *Help with incontinence.*

Other health checks

Looking after feet

Our feet are subjected to a lot of strain – sometimes even abuse – and it is worth offering to check on your relative's feet occasionally, and/or arranging chiropody visits. Remember that, as people get older, so their feet may alter. Old shoes, or new shoes in the size they have taken all their lives, may not be suitable. Look out for complaints such as bunions, corns and chilblains: in fact, any abnormality such as discoloration or flaking or thickening of the skin.

You should be able to access NHS chiropodists in your relative's area by consulting the GP. If your relative wants private chiropody, look in the telephone directory but check what qualifications the chiropodist has. Not all private chiropodists are State Registered. There may be an Age Concern toenail cutting service in the area – enquire from Age Concern or social services. All volunteers carrying out the nail cutting should have received training in hygiene and safe practice.

Eye care

Offer to arrange to have your relative's sight tested at least every two years. It is important that the eye test includes a check for the eye disease glaucoma, because it is most common in older people – especially if they are of African origin. If your relative does not already have an optician, ask the neighbours if they can recommend one, or try Yellow Pages or Talking Pages. Ask the optician if they have expertise in dealing with older people – especially important if your relative is suffering from dementia. Whilst many high-street outlets now provide ready-made spectacles, these are not advisable if people do not also maintain their regular eye tests as well. However, if your relative has misplaced their spectacles, they can provide a quick stop-gap until the prescription spectacles can be replaced. In fact, if your relative is very dependent on their spectacles and prone to misplacing them, it could be advisable to leave a spare pair of these cheaper spectacles with a neighbour.

Incidentally, if your relative has poor eyesight, and has net curtains at the window, try to persuade them to get rid of the curtains, as they filter out a lot of helpful light. If your relative's sight deteriorates markedly, contact organisations such as the Royal National Institute for the Blind (RNIB) for help and advice: the address is given on page 124.

Care of hearing

Try to note if your relative has the television sound turned up more than previously, or if they have to ask you to repeat yourself. If you suspect problems, offer to arrange for them to speak to the GP, as it could be something relatively simple and treatable, such as wax in the ear.

If, as a result of tests, it is recommended that they wear a hearing aid, there are various options available, including National Health aids and private ones. If your relative does have a hearing aid fitted, do not forget to look at the suitability of their phone, doorbell, and so on. Ask the district nurse to show you how to check and clean hearing aids.

Helpful information is available from the Royal National Institute for Deaf People (RNID), the address of which is given on page 124.

Dental care

Regular dental checks should be carried out, whether your relative has their own teeth or dentures. It may be important in checking that all the tissues in the mouth – not just the teeth – are still healthy, as mouth cancer becomes increasingly common as people get older. Some dentists will carry out home visits where necessary.

For more *information*

ⓘ Age Concern England Factsheet 5 *Dental care in retirement.*

Regular general practice check-ups are available

If your relative is 75 or over, they should be offered an annual health check from their doctor's surgery: find out when and where this will take place. All surgeries now produce leaflets giving details of their services. Also, you may wish to book a visit to the GP on one of your visits around October for the annual flu vaccination they should offer to older people in high-risk groups, which prevents illness in about 75 per cent of those vaccinated. These vaccinations need to be ordered in advance, so contact the GP practice in July or August to discuss whether your relative needs one.

Note It is important to remember that, whatever aspect of your relative's health you are looking at, they may choose to ignore your help or advice – and have a right to do so, no matter how frustrating this is for you. For example, you, or the GP, may encourage someone who has smoked for 60 years but who now has bronchitis and emphysema, to stop smoking. They may reject this advice – and you must accept their right to choose.

Mental health problems

If your relative seems confused, do not assume that they are suffering from dementia. An 'acute confusional state' can be caused by many factors, including infection, diabetes, dehydration or medication. Contact the GP to seek an accurate diagnosis.

Dementia

The mental health of your relative may need to be observed on visits. It is estimated that around 5 per cent of people over 65 and 20 per cent of those over 85 suffer from some degree of dementia. Dementia is not actually caused by old age or stress, although at stressful times the symptoms may become apparent as the person is confused by changes to a daily routine. The early stages of dementia may manifest themselves as forgetfulness, repetition of conversations, mislaying things or over-reaction to minor issues. Later, there may be incidents where the person becomes lost, forgets to eat or forgets they have eaten, or neglects their personal hygiene. Later stages may include incontinence, wandering, impaired speech and not recognising friends and family. If you notice any of the signs of what might be the earlier stages of dementia in your relative, don't panic. Many people with dementia can continue to live in their own environment for years.

For more *information*

🛈 A wide range of support and information is available from the Alzheimer's Disease Society (address on p 119).

🛈 Health Education Authority booklet *Who cares? Information and support for the carers of confused people.*

🛈 *Carers' Handbook* series: *Caring for someone who has dementia* published by Age Concern Books.

Depression

Although dementia is a common mental health problem, it would be wrong to talk about caring at a distance without mentioning depression, and the sensitive topic of suicide – not a comfortable subject to tackle. If your relative is lonely, there may be a risk of depression. This can be made worse if your relative's routine has centred on caring for their partner, who then dies.

The key differences between the signs of dementia and of depression are that people with depression are withdrawn and sad for long periods, whereas those with dementia may have more changeable mood swings. In both conditions there may be loss of the ability to concentrate, but with dementia the person is unlikely to be able to concentrate on anything in particular, whereas with depression the person may recognise and complain of their lack of concentration. Signs of depression to look for include lethargy, irritability, taking less pride in themselves or a lack of interest in things, diminishing appetite and disturbed sleep patterns. These could also, of course, be indicative of dementia, so, if there are changes in behaviour, it is best to seek professional help from the GP, who is trained to know what to do when someone becomes depressed.

Suicide

You may be surprised to learn that the suicide rate is greatest in people over 75, who are particularly at risk if they have been bereaved recently. Therefore any hint of suicidal thoughts must be taken seriously. Remember that depression is a treatable condition – but do not believe the 'old wives' tale' that people who talk about suicide never commit it. Sadly, over two-thirds of those who commit suicide have talked about it in general terms. Do not be put off talking about it if necessary – there is no evidence to suggest that asking someone about suicide makes it more likely.

If you need help to handle such a situation, or even if you just need to discuss your worries or suspicions, the GP or Samaritans may help.

Dealing with your relative's medicines

Joy

'It's a wonder Dad hadn't killed Mum, the cocktail of drugs he was giving her.'

'He was certain he was giving her the prescribed doses, but they were in fact the wrong drugs. He had the two most important ones muddled up. She was getting a double dose of Digoxin, which slows the heartbeat down, and he was giving her his aspirin tablets, which were the very things the GP said she must not take. Then we found she hadn't had any of her very strong painkillers. No wonder she was in so much pain.'

How to check the medication

Make sure you check all medication on every visit if your relative is confused. Depending on the nature of any problems, you could try encouraging systems such as putting out the day's pills in the morning, organising a special divided container clearly marked with the days and times that the tablets are to be taken (ask the pharmacist); obtaining bottles without the difficult-to-open child-proof caps; or asking the home help or district nurse to put the medication into the day's container each morning. Points to look out for include the expiry dates on any medicines (return out-of-date or unwanted medicines to the pharmacy), and the date of issue, the prescribed dose, the number of tablets remaining in the bottle, and whether they are in the original container.

Making sure your relative is eating well

How to check

On your visits, try to notice if your relative appears to be eating well. It could prove useful to offer to weigh them regularly.

There may be many reasons why they are not eating regularly or sensibly, such as ill-fitting dentures, physical illness, dementia, depression, inability to shop or inability to use equipment safely. Or a deceased partner might have been the cook and the bereaved person has never learned how.

If you suspect that they may not be eating regularly in your absence, it could be worth making a discreet note of the food stocks in hand and comparing the list with the stocks on your next visit. Another pointer to look for is whether the oven and grill look as though they have been used.

Ibrahim

'I had to resort to subterfuge in the end to prove to myself in the first instance that he really wasn't eating.'

'Even though the physical signs were there for me to see, he still insisted he was eating regularly. He swore that they weren't the same tins as last time in the cupboard, but direct replacements. I ended up secretly marking the tins. When I told him, he did admit he might occasionally forget, and finally allowed me to organise meals-on-wheels.'

Maintaining food hygiene for your relative

Many people are aware of the general principles of food hygiene but perhaps somewhat lax in their own homes. However, as older people are extremely vulnerable to food poisoning – in extreme cases it can cause death – it is well worth trying to encourage sound hygiene practice.

Some practical tips you can adopt include providing empty yoghurt cartons and asking the milkman to use them to cover the milk bottle tops to prevent contamination from birds pecking through. If your relative sometimes forgets to bring in the milk in the morning it could be placed in a covered holder outside (although your relative may not remember that the milk is inside this).

Eggs are a particular source of salmonella poisoning; they should be stored in the fridge and eaten within three weeks of laying. Therefore it is particularly important that someone – yourself, the neighbour or home help – take note of this, as once removed from the box they mostly do not have a date stamp.

Ensure that stocks of foil and cling film are to hand, as they are invaluable tools in maintaining safe food practice. If not to hand, they are the kind of shopping item easily forgotten by your relative or their shopper.

Labels can help

As it is important to maintain good food hygiene in the fridge, it often helps to clearly label the shelves, for example the lowest shelf saying 'raw meat only.' A fridge and freezer thermometer is cheap to buy and will help you or any more regular visitors (eg home helps) monitor any potential hazards. (Current advice says that a fridge should be no more than 5°C and freezers should be –18°C or below.)

It could also help if you clearly label a chopping board – you may have to buy an extra one – for raw meat only. Your relative may think this is unnecessary as they may have always used just one board for all foods, and 'no harm has ever befallen me'. However, it is worth trying to persuade them not to mix the handling of raw and cooked meats. You may also need to label pet food dishes and utensils.

Checking dates is important

Something worth checking on every visit is the use-by dates on canned foods, packets, jars (including open ones) and freezer foods. Be especially vigilant about canned foods at Harvest Festival time! Well-meaning people may inadvertently donate out-of-date produce which is then distributed, often to older people.

Becky

'Mum was going to cook pork chops for us for dinner. Luckily I noticed how rancid the meat looked straight out of the freezer.'

'I had been congratulating myself on all the supportive checks I had been carrying out. It had never occurred to me over the years to look in the freezer. The pork was four years old! I was consumed with guilt – and a desire for self-preservation! I hastily suggested dining out, and the neighbour's marauding cat got the blame for stealing the pork!'

If you need to give your relative a reason for checking the freezer, why not offer to defrost it regularly on your visits? Ask whoever helps with the shopping to purchase frozen foods with the longest use-by dates, and to ensure that dated labels are used on any loose foods placed in the freezer; try also to arrange for any home help's duties to include cleaning the fridge and checking its contents.

Support services are available

Do not forget that some of the best support services around are related to meals for older people. Investigate local luncheon clubs, which not only provide food but also help maintain morale and self-esteem, and there is often transport available. You might also consider day care in a residential home, which includes lunch and/or tea; meals-on-wheels; private meals services; and home help services. If someone does the shopping for your relative, you could ask them to include in the shopping foods that need no preparation, such as cold meats, bread, cheese and fruit. Or, if your relative still likes to cook, try to arrange the visits at a meal-time so that cooking is carried out under supervision.

Also, do not forget your relative's support network. If a neighbour or friend visits regularly, why not ask them if they would mind dropping off a few groceries at the same time, and you will reimburse them?

Helping your relative to cope with shopping

If your relative is still doing their own food shopping, there may be schemes that might help; for example, some areas run their own food co-operatives where small portions can be bought. Local social services departments would probably know if there is one in your area. Local shopkeepers can also be helpful by selling small-er portions and giving personal service, and a few still offer a delivery service. Nowadays, some supermarkets operate a bus ser-vice to and from their store; it is well worth enquiring about this on one of your visits. In some areas there are social car schemes or 'dial-a-ride' services that can be used to travel to and from the shops: social services or the local library should be able to supply information. Or you could ask a group of your relative's neigh-bours about the possibility of setting up a car pool for travelling to the shops. More and more milk delivery people carry stocks of many foods other than milk, including bread, juice, eggs, potatoes, yoghurt and even chicken. Approach local schools to find out if they co-ordinate assisted shopping trips as part of their care stud-ies curriculum. Also, you may be able to arrange for a home help to accompany your relative on a regular shopping trip.

Preventing a bare store cupboard

Shopping to stock someone else's store cupboard or freezer can be difficult and may sometimes prove to be a budgeting challenge.

Many foods are nutritious and convenient to prepare: if any of them are new to your relative, try to introduce them onto the menu on one of your visits. An example of an excellent cupboard stand-by that may be new to your relative is peanut butter, which contains high levels of protein and fibre, and which was originally invented as an easily digested and nutrient-dense food for older people. (Note, though, that some people are allergic to peanuts.)

Marie-Thérèse

'Dad was always reluctant to give me a list of his requirements. I think he felt it would be too much of a bother. So I sat down and devised a sort of "master list" which I broke down into sections, such as cereals, drinks, vegetables. Underneath each heading I wrote various options. Then each time I was going shopping for him he chose at least one item from every section.'

Below are some suggestions for store cupboard basics to cover any potential 'gap' times such as bad weather and bank holidays:

- baked beans;
- soups;
- rice;
- pasta;
- packet instant potatoes;
- canned fruit;
- canned vegetables;
- canned meat;
- canned fish;
- porridge oats;
- UHT fruit juice;
- UHT milk;
- meal replacements (eg Complan);
- peanut butter.

- dried fruit;
- Marmite/Bovril spread;
- stock cubes;
- tinned milk puddings;
- instant dessert mixes;
- evaporated milk;
- cereals;
- malted milk drinks;
- bread (keeps well in freezer);
- ready meals (tinned, packet or frozen);
- treacle;
- frozen vegetables;
- jams;

47

For more *i*nformation

ⓘ *Healthy Eating on a Budget* published by Age Concern Books.

Pets are important

The health of a pet can be an added worry

Keeping pets is well known to be good for people. However, if you are trying to provide support for your relative from a distance, the care of the pet can be an added worry for you. Certainly you will need to look for any signs of neglect on each of your visits, and you may feel it wise to take the animal to the vet's on a regular basis for a check-up, perhaps quarterly. There are many useful long-lasting veterinary products available nowadays that may help if your visits are infrequent. For example, there is now a flea spray that will give a dog protection for three months and a cat for two months, and there are also longer-lasting worming products. These are available only from a vet, and may seem expensive, but buying cheaper and less effective products is really false economy when you are not available to administer them on a regular basis. If your relative is in a lower income bracket, find out if they have a vet in the area who gives discounts to pensioners, or contact the nearest People's Dispensary for Sick Animals (PDSA) branch (find the telephone number in the local directory).

If your relative is becoming forgetful about feeding the pet, you could try putting a large notice in the kitchen as a reminder. Incidentally, people with dementia sometimes do not recognise capitals or handwriting, but recognise lower case printing: not 'CAT' or 'DOG' but 'cat' or 'dog'. A clearly labelled pet bowl may also help.

Wendy

'Dad used to feed the budgie every day. I can only visit twice a week and didn't notice he'd forgotten.'

'I looked in the cage regularly and there seemed to be enough seed there, but as I'd never kept birds before I hadn't realised that the bowl was full of empty husks and not seed. The poor thing died and I still feel so guilty. Dad was so devoted to the bird that it was the last thing I imagined would be neglected.'

Help may be available

Sources of help with looking after the pet may be in the neighbourhood – a local school may be able to encourage a responsible child to help, perhaps as part of an award scheme; local youth organisations such as the Scouts may be able to help; the vet may know of charitable organisations that provide dog-walking services; or the library or Citizens Advice Bureau may have information. There is a national charity, the Cinnamon Trust, that has a network of volunteer 'pet helps' who can provide practical help and a pet fostering service when owners are faced with a spell in hospital. You could also contact social services, as neglect of a pet could indicate to them a need to provide care for your relative; some home help agencies will incorporate a reasonable amount of pet care in their staff's daily routines as part of the purchased package. These pet care services can also be purchased privately.

Insurance for the pet could be a wise investment. Perhaps you could choose it as a present for your relative. It is easy to imagine the expense of a major operation for the pet, but some people underestimate the costs involved in routine long-term treatment. Age Concern is one of the organisations that promote a pets' insurance.

When the situation has irrevocably broken down

Despite the help available, you may still feel that the animal's health is unduly affected by your relative's behaviour. You probably have little choice then other than to re-home the animal. If you are unable or unwilling to adopt it, you will need to contact the RSPCA or Cats' Protection League or similar organisation (the telephone numbers can be found in Yellow Pages under 'Animal Welfare Societies') or the Cinnamon Trust for their list of pet-friendly homes (address on p 120).

Gary

'It broke her heart to lose the cat she loved so much.'

'I had tried everything but the cat was getting frailer. I would buy more than enough cat food to last but wouldn't find any on my next visit. One day I actually found my aunt eating from a can, thinking it was a stew for her. In the end I could not bear to see the cat suffer any more, and I had it re-homed in an area a long way away so it was unlikely to wander back. That was important because I told my aunt that the cat had died. I know it was a lie but I don't think she would have coped with knowing that it had to be taken away from her – I think her grief would have been twice as bad. Maybe I shouldn't have lied, but I've found that being devious is sometimes the best way to get through some of these situations with her.

'The cat is apparently doing fine now, so I think what I did was justified.'

Note **If your relative needs to go into care, there may be no need to re-home the animal, as some care homes accept residents' own pets – and not just budgerigars and cats. Ask the homes directly, or contact the Cinnamon Trust for information (address on p 120).**

5 How to get the most out of your visits

Finding information in an area unfamiliar to you or dealing with professionals at a distance can be both difficult and daunting. The frustration of not knowing which way to turn, or dealing with agencies that may seem not to care, can be wearing. Planning and preparation are vital so that you do not waste valuable time on your visits.

This chapter provides practical advice about whom to contact and how. It gives a sample framework for a letter to professionals, which you can adapt to suit your situation. It also includes advice on dealing with rejection, if your relative refuses to co-operate or to use any of the services you have accessed.

You will also find useful information on getting the most out of your visits in Chapters 3 and 4, 'Minimising risks' and 'What to look for when you visit'.

Tom

'Decide why you need to visit, and what the priorities are: in other words, plan ahead.'

'I used to think of my visits as having very different functions, so I planned them in different ways. At first, when I realised that I was actually a carer and I needed to know more, all my visits revolved around finding out what was on offer in Mum's area, so I went to see every professional, every local shopkeeper, all the neighbours, and so on until I felt I was making informed decisions and had set up a good contact network. I'm a doctor and although I had the advantage of knowing where to look for a lot of information, I still found a lot of anomalies between different areas.

'I wrote letters and used the phone before travelling there so that I was armed with as much information, and wasted as little time, as possible.

'This took a good three months to organise, but it was time well spent. Now Mum has people to take her to routine places like the dentist's and I don't have to allocate as much time to go up and take her there. And by planning into my diary an annual meeting with her social worker we are looking at the situation together more proactively and, hopefully, preventing many potential crises.

'I know it's not practical for everyone, but I find it helpful to make my visits on different days, not just at weekends. You get a clearer picture of things. I also make sure I use some time on all my visits to carry out a few regular checks on her food, on the house, and so on.

'My sister tells me I can't organise all of this in the "clinical" manner in which I sort out things at work, but she's wrong. The greatest benefit has been that I can now spend more of my visits on what people call "quality time": spending time with Mum, really being able to listen to her, and taking her on trips out. We can actually enjoy being together.'

Why do you need to visit?

The main focus of your visits will alter according to the mental and physical health of your relative, and the support available in the area. You may find that you are finding information or setting up support networks at first, but you should spend less time on this once arrangements are in place.

Although this book provides information to help you maximise the benefits of your visits, and therefore explores many potential problems, do bear in mind that your relative's priority may not be practical support: they may simply need your company.

Finding relevant information

Paul

'I didn't have a clue about what services were available in my own area, let alone his.'

'I couldn't see how I was supposed to find out about things when I didn't know they existed. But in some ways this worked to my advantage, because I just kept asking the social worker, "Why not? Why isn't this service available?" To be quite honest, it made both her and me look more closely for other solutions – probably because I was so insistent that someone must be able to help. I simply worked on the age-old premise: if you don't ask, you don't get.

'There were times when I felt as though I would be labelled as a trouble maker. I could imagine them at the other end saying, "Oh no, not him again". But I had to know what's what – and Uncle James had a right to know.

'Finding out all the information is a bit like putting together a jigsaw, but there is an amazing sense of satisfaction when you complete the picture. And, to be fair, there was more help available than I had ever imagined. It's about knowing where to start and when not to stop.'

Getting information in an area unknown to you can seem to be an almost impossible task. You want to do some preparation before you arrive, but how? Bother the neighbours again? And are they likely to know the kind of information you need?

The standard help points of social services, Citizens Advice Bureau, Age Concern, library, carers' groups and so on remain some of the most useful sources of information in any area, and many provide impartial advice on potential sources of help for a huge range of things. Your local branches or groups may be able to give you details of those in your relative's area, if you have not already obtained them on a previous visit.

At least some of your early visits will probably be best spent in getting to know the capabilities of local organisations, shops, and so on. The following list gives an at-a-glance guide for getting information about key professional services:

Service	Access via
Meals-on-wheels	Social services or GP
Home care	Social services; private agencies
District nurses, community psychiatric nurses (CPNs), health visitors, continence advisers	GP
Occupational therapists	Social services
Social workers	Social services
Residential or nursing homes	Social services; health authority
Chiropodists	GP; private chiropodist practices
Hobby clubs, societies, classes	Social services; library; local care homes; local Age Concern group
Luncheon clubs	Social services; library; local Age Concern group

Who are the professionals?

Chiropodists provide treatment and advice about foot care. Remember to enquire about their qualifications.

Community psychiatric nurses (CPNs) are trained nurses who specialise in supporting and advising patients with mental health problems and their families in the community.

Continence advisers are qualified nurses with specialist training in the provision of advice on toileting problems.

District nurses are qualified nurses with further training in practical nursing of people in their own homes.

Health visitors are registered nurses who have taken extra training in providing advice on health care. In some areas they deal only with children's health, in others with the health of children and of older people.

Home care assistants provide practical help and support in the home. They may also have other titles such as 'home helps' or 'community assistants'. They may be employed by social services or a private company: in the case of the latter look for a company that is a member of the United Kingdom Homecare Association (UKHCA – address on p 125).

Occupational therapists (OTs) are trained to provide assessment and advice on mobility and aids.

Social workers are trained to provide assessment of and support in the care needs of individuals and their families.

Supplementary services

You may decide to look for supplementary support services for your relative; for example, a laundry collection service, whereby someone calls weekly at your relative's house to collect and launder sheets. Social services will normally be the most useful source of information on the various services available in the locality, whether sponsored by them or available privately. However, one of the easiest ways to find out about any particular service in another area is to use Talking Pages, which is now free by telephoning 0800 600 800. You simply ask for, say, laundries or dry cleaners in a certain area, or home help services. Admittedly you will be given a random selection of numbers – but if you were looking in the local Yellow Pages yourself and did not have prior knowledge of any of the companies, you would still be making a random choice.

Questions to ask

If you are planning on accessing services from any organisation such as a home care service whereby strangers will be entering your relative's home, you may wish to ask the following questions of the company:

- How many staff do they employ?
- How do they check their backgrounds?
- What are their selection criteria for staff (qualifications, experience)?
- Do you need to pay an hourly rate or flat rate per task?
- Do you pay extra for travel costs?
- Are these rates inclusive of VAT?
- How do they carry out an assessment of a person's care needs?
- Is the agency a member of the United Kingdom Homecare Association (UKHCA)?
- Can they provide domestic and/or personal care?
- Are they insured in case of accident/damage?
- Will they provide continuity of service over holiday/sickness periods?
- Is there a 24-hour office contact service?

Get the answers to your questions in writing before you take up any services, to make sure that there are no misunderstandings.

Contacting professionals for help

Whether your relative contacts professionals for help or asks you to do so, the following information may be of help. The suggestions and comments here assume that your relative has accepted your offer to do this.

Nsiki

'There's just one big word: frustration.'

'When you are trying to find out things in another area, it is so easy to be fobbed off on the telephone because you don't have your wits about you. I know how easy it is – I do the same to people on the phone in my own job! But it really is frustrating for the person at the other end to be told "I'm sorry they're not available, can I take a message?" I also find it a bit annoying trying to talk to professionals when they use jargon. I found out the names for services on offer in my own area, only to discover that in my parents' area everything had a different title.'

Obtaining information from official sources can be difficult enough in person, but is even more so at a distance. Trying to fit your visiting schedule around that of professionals such as geriatricians or social workers making domiciliary visits is very difficult. Even trying to make an appointment to see them can be frustrating, and the result may be that it is impossible for you to make face-to-face contact on one of your visits.

Even trying to obtain information from hospitals, if your relative has been admitted there, can be daunting.

Zoë

'Visiting hospitals at weekends is maddening!'

'I can only visit at weekends because of work commitments, and this was fine until mother went into hospital for several weeks. My weekend visits took on an extra element of frustration as there was seldom anyone on duty who could give me the information I needed – or so it seemed – to make a decision. And when I tried to ring during the week, they always sounded too busy to talk to me and I ended up being fobbed off with the standard phone replies instead of the information I really wanted.'

Preparation is the key

Many of us do not make the most of our phone calls, and waste time and money. The best way to obtain the information you need is to plan.

Make a list of your objectives: what do you need to know from them? What might they need to know about you or your relative? Write down some key facts, as even basic details such as someone's age might escape you at the time. Remind yourself to ask them by what date you might expect to hear back from them. If you feel nervous about phoning, you could write out everything you want to say to them in advance and read from your paper; for example, 'My name is ... and I am the daughter of ... who is one of your clients. The reason I am ringing is to inform you that ...', and so on.

Telephone techniques

If you do not know the name of the person you need to speak to, try to ascertain that first from the receptionist who answers: there is nothing more time-consuming than going into great detail about a given situation, only to find that the telephonist has to transfer you. If the person you need to speak to is not available, make sure you write down the date, the time and the name of any other person you speak to – and ask for your call to be returned. In fact, it is a good idea to keep a log of all the dates, times and names of telephone calls.

You should also make a written note of any information you are given. Reserve judgement on what is relevant to your situation until much later – and if anyone suggests or confirms anything by telephone, always ask for them to follow it up in writing. You may also want to follow up the phone call with your own written confirmation of the content of the call. This can help prevent later misunderstandings.

If anyone uses 'professional jargon', do not under any circumstances be afraid to ask for clarification of the terms used, no matter to whom you are speaking. Also, do not be afraid at any point in the conversation to ask for a few moments just to refer back to the notes you have made: do not worry about the silence. If you feel nervous about making 'official' phone calls, stand up while using the telephone: it really does make you feel more assertive!

If you want what you say to be held on record, for example if you are making a complaint, a letter is usually better than a phone call.

Writing official letters

You may prefer or need to make contact with officials by letter. It can be very easy to fall into the trap of writing a lengthy document that reflects your difficulties or frustrations, but you risk missing key points so it may be better to make your first letter fairly brief. If your relative is unlikely to be able to give background information, you can offer to supply further details by telephone or in writing. (Your relative's religion, hobbies or previous work can prove vital in helping a professional such as a social worker put together an appropriate package of care or even to access sources of funding for them.)

It can be helpful for the person replying to your letter if you number the paragraphs in your letter. If you are responding to a letter sent to you or your relative, quote any reference number given, which might look something like 'Ref. ANO/123'.

Two important points about writing 'official' letters:

■ If you have difficulty in writing these letters (as many people have), contact an organisation such as the Citizens Advice Bureau for help.
■ Always keep a copy for your records.

A sample framework to adapt

The following letter can be adapted to your own circumstances:

Your Address

Date

Dear Mr X

Re: Mrs A N Other, of [address]

My aunt, Mrs A N Other, has asked me to write to ask you for details of home care services available for her. She lives alone and is finding it increasingly difficult to manage her personal care, as well as her domestic tasks. Her neighbours are also voicing their concerns about her safety. I am unable to visit frequently and am therefore unable to give regular support.

I enclose personal details about my aunt on a separate sheet. Please keep me informed about any assessment visits, etc. I can be contacted at the above address by phone on 0111 666 666 between 9am and 5pm weekdays.

I plan to visit my aunt during the week commencing [date], and would therefore like an appointment to meet you personally to discuss the situation and options available.

Yours sincerely

C D Anyone

Key points, such as those given below, could either be included in the main body of the letter in numbered paragraphs or given on a separate sheet.

Mrs A N Other

Address

Date of birth

Age

Widowed; lives alone in council property.

Has a pet dog. Struggling to look after it.

Greatest difficulty appears to be walking up the stairs. (Toilet is upstairs.)

One neighbour available to do a little shopping.

Appears to be having difficulty in administering own medication but does not recognise this.

In receipt of Income Support.

Ex-servicewoman; also worked at XYZ department store.

Personal contact

On one of your visits, you may need to meet personally with someone such as a social worker or GP. The advice given in the telephone techniques section on planning ahead – working out in advance what you want to say – and writing down what you aim to achieve applies equally to meetings in person. If you do not feel confident about the meeting, it is perfectly acceptable to take a friend or relative with you for moral support.

When making the appointment to be seen, you may find it useful to ask for details of parking facilities nearby, or the distance from the nearest public transport stop. The last thing you want is to be late and find they have not been able to wait for you.

Staying in control

Whatever method of communication you are using, the following hints apply:

- Be persistent. You are not a nuisance.
- You have a right to obtain information to help your relative.
- Say 'No' if you feel you are being pressured into providing more support than you can really give.
- Stay calm. Anger begets anger and usually gets nowhere.
- If you are unhappy with the outcome, follow the complaints procedure, which all official bodies have in place.

One final note: depending on many circumstances, including the mental health of your relative, you may find that the professional with whom you are dealing simply cannot disclose certain information to you and may propose discussing matters with them directly. Your relative has a right to this.

What to do if your relative refuses help

Lisa

'She chooses to live in squalor with no support. I feel so ashamed.'

'I know that others think it's appalling the state Mum is in, and that I neglect her – but if only they knew. I spent ages finding out what was available; the social worker visited and tried to persuade her to accept some help, but she chooses to live in that old house with no running water and an outside toilet. She's certainly more confused nowadays, but she's not harming anyone else, so the social worker and I had to back off and let her get on with it. I'm sure she'll end up killing herself one day: I imagine her slipping on the ice going outside to the loo, and not being able to get any help. The only thing I've managed to set up is for the woman at the farm nearby to call in every morning just to say, "hello". Luckily she is thick-skinned, as Mum always has a few choice words for her about minding her own business.'

Dealing with the emotions

It can be extremely galling to set up all sorts of support and help, only to find that it is spurned by your relative. You may have suspected this might happen but hoped you could persuade them otherwise, or it may have occurred unexpectedly. Their perception of their situation and priority needs may differ immensely from yours.

Sociologists say that it is a basic human need to feel wanted, so having to deal with rejection can be particularly hurtful. This can be worse if you have worked hard to find out about, or to arrange, help, and it is normal if you feel exasperation, frustration, a sense of failure or sheer anger. However, it is worth remembering that your relative could be experiencing the same range of emotions. There may be frustration at not being able to cope; exasperation at your attempts to 'interfere'; anger that you are trying to make decisions for them or that they are out of control of the situation. They may feel ashamed about their circumstances and unwilling to reveal them to others.

What can you do?

As with many situations, it is vital to step back and ask yourself, 'Who is this a problem for?' If your relative is coping, albeit at a level that is perhaps lower than before or than you would prefer, and if they choose to live in a certain manner or to refuse services, you will probably find that professionals such as social workers will agree that they should be allowed to continue – whatever the neighbours may think!

Most people are prepared to give up many things and risk illness or injury to stay in their own homes. The problem arises when a professional has to make a decision about what is an 'acceptable' level of risk, or when a client becomes an immediate danger to themselves or to others (see 'Legal implications' on p 64). There can be a fine line between supporting someone's situation and stifling their independence and freedom of choice.

Dealing with their worries

Listen carefully to your relative's anxieties. Give reassurance, and be prepared to compromise: perhaps you have offered them too much too soon? They may be secretly worried about the cost of services, or too proud to accept your financial help, in which case you could offer it as a Christmas or birthday gift. Try to persuade them to accept 'no-obligation trial periods' of services. You may have to plan a visit to accompany them to view day care facilities, for example (although social workers can usually do this for you). Look for alternatives that could fulfil the same function as your original rejected suggestion.

Lee

'Mum refused to have meals-on-wheels because she saw it as "going on the welfare". But it was crucial for her to have meals delivered because we had had to disconnect the cooker after she had set fire to the kitchen. My friend owns a rather posh restaurant and kindly offered to supply her with a hot meal every day. She pays her bill weekly, and the meals are delivered by taxi. She was more than happy to accept this, and in fact it suits her better because the other meals were scheduled for lunch time whereas these are in the evening, and she has always eaten her main meal of the day at about 8pm.'

If your relative still does not listen to your suggestions, it may help for someone else to talk to them, such as their GP or minister.

Not what but how?

Your relative may not be rejecting what you are doing, but how you are doing it. For example, when you carry out a task for your relative it may be your methods that they object to.

Sheila

'Often when I suggest or do something, Dad will say, "No, don't do it like that. Mum always used to do it this way ..." Frustrating though it may be, I try not to let it cause an argument, and accept it as a fond memory of Mum for Dad rather than a bone of contention. Often I know I could do something better or quicker but does it really matter? If I do it his way he's more likely to accept the help.'

Even if your offers of help are still rejected, continue to gather information and plan ahead so that you are prepared if the day comes when they accept the services that are available.

Legal implications

Under section 47 of the National Assistance Act 1948 or guardianship under the Mental Health Act 1983, it is possible for someone to be removed from their own home and admitted into care, if they are deemed to be a danger to themselves, and perhaps to others as well. It is very rare, though, for professionals to enforce decisions by actions such as these; this is done only in extreme circumstances. It is vital that older people retain the ability to make choices for themselves: in the words of Age Concern, 'Choice is not ours to give or allow, but is ours to promote and facilitate.'

For more *i*nformation

ⓘ Carers National Association Factsheet *A Fair Deal for Carers – Your guide to getting services.*

ⓘ *The Carer's Handbook: What to do and who to turn to* published by Age Concern Books.

ⓘ Improve your negotiating/assertiveness skills: look in the business section of the local library for relevant books.

6 Looking after yourself

Caring while sharing a household with your relative is widely acknowledged as potentially difficult and stressful. However, caring at a distance can present its own problems and pressures and take an emotional toll on you.

There may be factors unique to the distance situation such as taking time off work to travel to your relative, or feeling the need to spend all of your holidays with them. Travelling back and forth may be very tiring. You may feel an increased level of stress and guilt because you are unable or unwilling to be in closer proximity to them.

This chapter examines some of the emotions you may experience, and sets out some practical ideas for you to explore.

Formal assessment of your needs

Under the Carers (Recognition and Services) Act 1995 and the Disabled Persons (Services, Consultation and Representation) Act 1986, social services departments should carry out a separate assessment of carers' ability to provide care (existing carers who provide, and those who intend to provide, a substantial amount of care on a regular basis). For people caring at a distance, the key word is frequency, but local authorities are likely to decide what constitutes substantial and regular – which implies regular intervals but not necessarily the frequency. Therefore if, for example, your distance caring is a daily visit and you are experiencing problems, it may be worth asking for your own separate assessment if you have requested an assessment for your relative.

It is worth noting that, although the Act obliges social services to take into account the carer's assessment when deciding what services the older/disabled person requires, it does not give the carer an automatic right to any service provision. Depending on your individual circumstances, you may find that you can have your own needs (eg to have regular breaks) taken into consideration in a formal assessment of the person you are caring for. Criteria used for assessment include:

- high risk or vulnerability of the person being cared for or their carer;
- a high level of stress experienced by the person being cared for or their carer;
- a high level and duration of assistance being given;
- specifically and reasonably requested by the person being cared for and their carer.

Kathy

'I knew there were sources of help. But I didn't want to let social services know.'

'I was brought up to believe that, once a social worker was involved, you were somehow labelled as a problem family and that society would look down on you. Mum had an archaic view that you would never contact "the welfare" unless you were absolutely desperate – which in her case meant that you would never do so.

'So although I was told by friends that social services could help me, I didn't even consider it. After all, it wasn't as if Mum was actually living with me: I was only visiting once a day. So our case wasn't desperate, was it? It took a near nervous breakdown and my doctor's support to make me realise the stress I had been under – that I was feeling desperate for help – and that there was no shame in admitting it, or in getting help from social services.

'The social worker was absolutely marvellous in helping me to understand the scope of his work nowadays. He organised a package of care for Mum and put me in touch with a carers' group where I found out I wasn't the only person in the world in the same situation, which was the way it had begun to seem. He was also very tactful when he heard me explaining to Mum that he was a nurse. He didn't actually lie to her himself, he simply didn't contradict me or offer her any more information about his job. We are all taught not to lie, but there are times when it is justified. She would never have agreed to any contact with him otherwise, and the situation would have deteriorated.'

Acknowledging your feelings

People caring at a distance may not expect to be affected by stress. They may feel that only those who live with an older person are likely to suffer. However, it is important to acknowledge that the stress of trying to help someone and not being able to be there in person can be enormous.

You may also worry about becoming ill and not being able to visit or telephone your relative, with no one being aware of this. To alleviate this worry you can carry a card with wording such as, 'I am a carer and I visit my mother daily. In case of my illness or accident please contact [name and telephone number]'. Get permission of the person in your relative's support network before you list their name and telephone number in this way.

Stress

It is important to remember that stress is one's own personal reaction to pressure. Some people will cope better than others with varying degrees of pressure, and indeed in the short term the effects of stress can help them make decisions within a given timescale. However, constant stress is debilitating, and all carers must place their own well-being high on their list of priorities. If this means taking a holiday that does not, for once, involve visiting your relative, your need for the break should override any feelings of guilt. If you become ill because you have not taken a rest, you will be totally unable to help your relative. (Some compromise solutions are discussed later in this chapter.)

Warning signs

Potential warning signs of stress include inability to sleep, headaches, tiredness, depression, irritability, eating more or less than usual, or possible psychosomatic illnesses such as eczema. Looking after your own health means not ignoring any symptoms and making time to go to your GP, no matter how busy you are.

Actions you can take

Your action plan for dealing with the stress may well include the following:

1 Be honest with yourself about the cause.
2 If you can do something about the cause, do it now. If not, look for ways to deal with it and to relax. This may be as simple as booking one night a week in your diary to go out and socialise, to swim or to practise yoga. Relaxation is a learned skill, but a good long-term way to help combat stress. Do not cut yourself off from friends, relatives and hobbies, whatever the time pressures may be.
3 If you have to deal with a crisis and therefore feel stressed, follow the 'SOS': sigh out slowly (and loudly!) while dropping your shoulders. This really does help.
4 Defuse any stressful anticipation of having to cope with emergencies by attending a relevant course to address your fears, for example a first aid course.
5 If you are feeling angry about the caring situation, acknowledge that this is normal. It may help to talk to a professional such as a social worker, GP, minister or counsellor, or you could telephone the Relaxation for Living Trust (01983 868 166).

6 Contact a carers' support group, through social services contacts, Carers National Association (address on p 120) or the local library information service. Almost everyone benefits from having someone to talk to who is empathetic to their situation.

7 Tell yourself it may be difficult to cope, but you have coped before and will again.

8 Do not feel that you have to go on for ever – or that you need to be perfect!

9 Laughter is the best medicine – try to laugh off the more minor problems and save your energies for any major crises.

10 Do not be pressured into things you really do not want to do. Learn to say 'No'. Look out for assertiveness or stress control courses advertised in the newspapers or at local colleges.

For more *information*

i Your GP may be able to refer you for counselling on the NHS. Alternatively, contact the British Association for Counselling for approved local practitioners (address on p 120).

Experiencing feelings of guilt

Sarah

'I was riddled with guilt from the minute I realised they weren't coping well.'

'Guilt that I hadn't noticed before. Guilt that I had let their situation deteriorate so badly. Guilt that I could not be with them often, because I needed my job so badly to pay the mortgage. And, worst of all, guilt because I myself am a social worker. Then professional pride came into the emotional baggage. What if fellow professionals in the care industry – my parents' social workers – were criticising me for all the things I already felt guilty about?'

Guilt is a natural emotion. It may be caused by many factors, and can be made worse when caring at a distance because you are simply not physically able to help in many circumstances. However, guilt must not be allowed to become out of proportion to everything else. There may well be feelings of guilt about how you are coping with various practical issues, but there may be other deep-rooted feelings.

Neslihan

'I feel guilty because my sister copes so well with Dad all year round and I only have him for holidays – and when he's here I get so irritated by stupid little things like the way he chomps his food. It makes me sound terrible, doesn't it? I know it's no big deal, but if I'm honest he has always annoyed me – and vice versa. That's why I know it would never work for him to live with us.'

Negative feelings are normal and permissible

There may be some situations where you may not, if you are honest with yourself, even like your relative very much. After all, in any family setting some members are closer than others, and it may be that this person had attitudes or habits previously which you didn't actually like. Before you let guilt interfere with objective decision-making, it is important to recognise your own feelings and permit them. For example, you may be considering living together with your relative, perhaps both selling up and buying a larger property, or having them move into your present property. Before you take any such major decision, ask yourself truthfully if you can really live with them. Allow yourself to say 'No'.

Give credit where it is due: to you!

If you continue with your distant caring and your relative's situation breaks down, so that they are neglecting themselves or their home, it is possible that you will feel some guilt. Recognise the strain you are under and accept that you may feel helpless. How-

71

ever, if you have done everything in your power to support them, and they choose to live in that way, or are still relatively content and not endangering others, you should feel a sense of pride that you have enabled them to continue to retain some freedom of choice, control over their lives, and therefore independence. Give yourself the credit you are due for doing your utmost to help.

For more *i*nformation

i Alzheimer's Disease Society Advice Sheet 17 *Dealing with guilt.*

Discovering the positive aspects

Inevitably, because this book aims to help in crisis situations, it focuses on many of the potential negative aspects of caring from a distance. However, in looking after yourself, try to focus on the positive aspects.

Barry

'I've given up arguing and don't feel guilty about taking the money.'

'Every time we visit – about once a month – she cancels the home carer. This used to anger and bemuse me, but she always then tried to pay me the petrol money for my visit in recompense. I've given up arguing now. When I do the work the home carer does at other times, it makes me feel I've done a little bit towards supporting her. And I've come to appreciate that it allows her to express her appreciation in a tangible way and that is important to her. So to be honest I am never out of pocket because of my visits.'

Mark

'It's got its nice bits. Father writes out the cheque to cover my flight each time. I no longer feel guilty. Of course I would visit anyway, but he really feels happier doing this, than if he were "beholden" to me.'

Although not every older relative can afford or is inclined to sub-sidise someone's visits, it may be a moral dilemma you need to work through. If you are covering your out-of-pocket expenses and they feel better about making a financial contribution, it may help ease the pressure all round if you accept. It is also worth noting that even the law acknowledges that there may be need for reim-bursement of expenses in some cases: carers with Enduring Power of Attorney are entitled to cover out-of-pocket expenses from their relative's finances.

For more *i*nformation

i See Chapter 7, 'Dealing with your relative's finances'.

Responding positively

Melissa

'The tears when I'm leaving aren't as bad as I thought they would be. I've learned to look at them as a sort of "bonding" between us: a confirmation of how we feel about each other. If we lived nearer each other we might well take each other's emotions and love for granted, and never express it – the kind of guilt feeling many people have on bereavement. At least I know that we have said how much we love each other.'

Kelly

'I've cared for our old family friend for many years now. I know she needs to keep up the "stiff upper lip" image for her neighbours, but this means that she seems to save up all her moans and groans – and her tears – for me. But I'm prepared for this, and I take it as a compliment that she feels secure enough with me to "let go".'

Try to look at the more positive aspects of situations that you may initially find distressing. As these carers show, if you examine the situation, tears from your relative need not always make you feel emotionally drained or guilty.

Coping with caring and work

People who live with their older relatives may have a need to retain their own work, be that a financial or emotional need or both. If you are caring at a distance, you may have the same needs, and there can be particular effects on your work directly because of the distance factor.

Solomon

'I always visited my sister on my days off. I thought it wasn't affecting my work, but it was – indirectly.'

'Although I never took any time off for the visits, the tiredness I felt from using up all my spare time on long drives to visit her took their toll. I had to balance my home life and work priorities with the need to visit, but my visits became more infrequent and therefore more intense and tiring each time. One of my managers simply said I had to sort myself out and stop coming to work dog-tired after my weekends off. The other was more sympathetic to my situation but because of the pressure of work was unable to "carry" me. So I ended up taking an extra day's annual leave after each weekend visit. The alternative was to lie and call in sick at times, but I could never do that.'

Companies vary in their attitudes to supporting distant carers. Some, such as some of the major banks, have an excellent reputation for their supportive approach, for example allowing flexi-time, but others do not have the inclination or indeed the flexibility to do so. Good companies may well have 'compassionate leave' arrangements in their terms and conditions of employment. Do try to save this for an absolute crisis – do not use it for a 'semi-emergency': you may need it later on. In today's economic climate with tight profit margins for many, it can be difficult for companies to offer the support they might wish to give to carers. However, this does not alter the fact that one of the pressures on you may be the emotional strain of balancing work and personal priorities.

It is important to find out in advance your company's policies with regard to this kind of need. Consult your line manager, personnel manager, occupational health department or trade union as applicable. If you belong to a trade union, if necessary ask them to negotiate with your company over their policies on time off for carers.

What do you need?

Carers' needs vary. For example, there may come a time when you need to finish early on a Friday to travel to your relative for a weekend visit. Or you may live near them and need to visit them every morning. Or it may be that there is no public telephone in the office but you need to ring your relative daily at lunch time. The most important thing is to negotiate with your boss: if you need to leave work early, make sure you make up the time, perhaps at lunch breaks or later on another day. Do not make surreptitious telephone calls: ask for permission to use the phone and pay for the calls.

Bosses are often sympathetic to carers' needs, but will welcome prior warning of issues where possible. Do not try to talk to your boss about such important matters 'on spec'. Write a note outlining your personal circumstances and ask for a specific appointment to discuss the practical issues. Remember, though, that your boss will need to work within corporate policies.

You may find it useful to contact the organisation Friends of Carers (address on p 122). Their aim is to raise awareness among employers about the caring responsibilities that many people have, and ways in which they can help. You may also decide to improve your own negotiation skills: the business section in any library will have books on this topic, or there may be courses at your local further education college.

For further *information*

ⓘ Contact New Ways to Work for advice on flexible work arrangements (address on p 124).

ⓘ Contact the TUC (Trades Union Congress: address on p 125).

Other work options

Despite having negotiated with your employer, you may still find that you need to re-appraise your working life because of the need to care at a distance. Can you afford to work part-time rather than full-time? Could this be a temporary solution or would it need to be permanent? Is job-sharing an option? Could you take a period of unpaid leave? Or do you actually need to look for alternative employment? (Bear in mind that any alterations you make to your working life may affect your promotion prospects and/or pension entitlements.)

If you decide that you must find another job, you may feel that no one else will employ you if you tell them that your need for change is because of your personal commitments. However, this is a valid reason for change, and can be turned to your advantage if you point out to a prospective employer that balancing your work and personal commitments successfully demonstrates qualities such as an ability to plan and to organise.

Going into care

You and your relative may decide that the only way you can cope with your job is to have the reassurance that they are being cared for in a residential or nursing home. This may be the prime factor that precipitates their admission to a home. You will need to explore all the options, as the issue to be resolved is whether what is best for you is also best for them.

The importance of regular breaks

When you are trying to balance your home life with caring for a relative far away, holidays may seem to be the furthest thing from your mind. It is widely recognised that if you live with an older relative, you are likely to need a break away from them. It is also important to recognise that, if your caring is at a distance, much of your spare time is probably focused on some support, if not an actual visit, for your relative. You may also have your immediate family's holiday needs to attend to, and therefore a broad spectrum of ages, needs and abilities to cater for. You need to look after yourself, though; otherwise, if you have no break at all, you may not be in a position to provide support to others.

This section of the chapter covers taking holidays together or away from your relative, as well as organising holidays for them that also give you a break from your caring at a distance. Several options are open to you.

Staying at your relative's home

You may choose to spend most or all of your holidays at the home of your relative, which gives you an opportunity to carry out all the checks identified throughout this book, and perhaps to take your relative on outings as well. There is no doubt that outings could be extremely beneficial, as your relative may have little opportunity to see how the community has changed, or to view surrounding scenery or places of previous interest. If you do choose to spend your holidays at your relative's home, try to include, as well as the functional tasks, some social activities, no matter how small, such as taking photographs and then perhaps reminiscing over older pictures, or sharing news about recent events.

Do consider carefully whether it is wise to spend every holiday visiting. Sooner or later your immediate family will require your presence during holiday time, but you may have set a precedent you find hard to break.

77

Staying in accommodation nearby

Your relative may be delighted to have the opportunity to be your host for a holiday. However, it may be too disorientating or stressful for them to cope with house guests, or you may not wish to spend 24 hours a day with them, or there may simply be no room for you to stay. An alternative to consider is to book hotel or B&B accommodation near your relative's home. This can be especially useful if you are taking a young family with you to visit.

Staying at your home

A useful option may be to invite your relative to stay at your own home during your holidays. If getting time off from work is becoming difficult, you might invite your relative to stay with you and continue to go to work during the day. Obviously the feasibility of this depends on your relative's current condition, but may prove to be the most effective solution if, for example, you have two older people (perhaps your parents) and one is in effect the primary carer of the other. It can provide an excellent compromise, in that you do not have to take extra time off work or use up your holidays, but your relatives have a change of scenery, with trips out in the evenings and weekends. Inevitably, though, there could be drawbacks as well as advantages.

Hywel

'We weren't prepared, so the first two days were sheer hell.'

'Dad was totally confused at night, wandering and shouting. My wife and I got no sleep and were prepared to take him home after two days, as we were at work each day and needed our sleep. Also, Dad mistook our bedroom for the toilet and you can guess what happened. However, a friend suggested some practical things to help, and the visit proved to be successful. Next time we'll be prepared in advance for all eventualities. You need to look after yourself; otherwise, if you end up having no break at all, you may not be in a position to provide support to others.'

The change of scenery may prove to be disorientating, especially at night, if your relative is experiencing any degree of dementia. In preparation for this, it may be useful to take some precautions in advance as necessary, such as:

- labelling doors such as the toilet and bedroom;
- plugging in a nightlight;
- putting a waterproof mattress protector on the bed;
- using luminous tape to guide the way from the bed to the toilet;
- taping over plugs not to be removed from their sockets (such as the freezer);
- putting a gate at the top of the stairs.

Bringing relatives to stay with you can also give you an opportunity to observe how one is caring for the other. You may spot a problem that can be more easily hidden within their own home – and therefore take appropriate action.

Louise

'At first I thought it was a total disaster to have them stay with me, but it gave me the opportunity to check out what was happening.'

'It was only when they were with me that I saw how bad the situation really was. At least I caught it in time. We found that she was tipping some of his medication away and not giving him any analgesia, and it turned out that he had a nasty varicose ulcer on his leg which she was dressing daily with a dry dressing, which was agony when she peeled it off. Mum was certainly giving attention to this but had not called in the doctor or nurse. Mind you, the saddest thing was that we found that Mum was experiencing a greater degree of dementia than we had realised.'

Note If your relative is receiving any regular medical treatment such as injections or dressings changed, arrangements can be made for the service to be provided by your local surgery: contact your relative's GP or district nurse in the first instance.

Respite care

You may also wish to consider bringing your relative to stay in a care home in your own district for a holiday: short breaks in care establishments are often referred to as respite care. The advantages include the knowledge that they are receiving professional care in what may be a hotel-like establishment, while minimising disruption to your home life or work schedule and, for them, the possible stimulation of a new environment, activities, and so on. However, depending on their mental state, the new environment and activities could prove to be disorientating and unsettling for them. Nevertheless, it is an option worth exploring.

Preparing for excursions

Even if mobility is maintained in their own home, you may find that on excursions out your relative cannot manage to walk far, or needs the toilet more frequently. Again, try to anticipate these possibilities and borrow/hire a wheelchair and such equipment as necessary: contact your local Red Cross branch. Other sources of help include the Women's Royal Voluntary Service (WRVS: the number will be in the phone directory) or local Shopmobility schemes (contact the council to find out if there is one in the area).

If there is the possibility of an incontinence problem with your relative, it is useful to pack in the car a discreet box of waterproof seat covering, wet wipes, perhaps cardboard urinal bottles, a blanket to help maintain privacy/discretion in the need to use the bottles, paper towels, tissues, and possibly a change of clothing. All this can be done in advance so that if the need doesn't arise your relative will never know about it; if any of these measures is needed, though, they will probably be glad of the quiet and orderly support without a fuss or panic.

There is a scheme operated by RADAR whereby keys for public toilets that are adapted for disabled people are made available. MAVIS can give advice on alterations to your vehicle to accommodate a disabled person. It may also be worthwhile finding out from the local council about the 'orange badge scheme' which allows you to park your car on yellow lines when your relative is a passenger.

For more *i*nformation

i Contact the British Red Cross (address on p 120).

i Contact RADAR (address on p 124).

i Contact MAVIS (address on p 123).

i Contact the local council for details of the 'orange badge scheme'.

Travelling to the holiday

If your relative is coming to your home to spend a holiday with you, you will need to look carefully at travel arrangements. If you are collecting them by car, you may need to prepare as outlined on page 80 for excursions, and to make careful note of the distances between service stations: refer to a map, the AA or RAC. If you live in the London area you may find that you can book a taxi at a reasonable rate for your relative: there may be concessions available. If they are to travel by coach, on long-distance journeys there may be a steward who can be asked to keep an eye on them. If travelling by train, arrangements can be made in advance for facilities such as a portering service and wheelchairs at the stations of departure and arrival. Of course, if the travel entails a flight, air cabin crew can be briefed about any special needs. The British Red Cross can often give advice about and help with travel arrangements for a special journey.

Whatever the mode of travel, do not be afraid to state your relative's needs: after all, this is the age of customer service/ charters/commitment, to name but three jargon phrases. There are also an increasing number of specialist transport schemes which, although usually operating only within a local area, may be bookable for longer trips, for example to transport your relative to and from your home or to another holiday destination. Investigate these in both your relative's and your own geographical areas – details are usually available from social services.

For more *information*

ⓘ Contact the local Disablement Information and Advice Line (DIAL) for information and advice for disabled people planning to travel (central office address on p 121).

ⓘ Contact the local WRVS for information about the availability of escort taxis (telephone number in the local directory).

ⓘ Contact Tripscope for transport information and help in planning your journey (address on p 125).

ⓘ Contact Holiday Care Service for detailed information about national charities that give grants towards holidays (address on p 122).

Holiday suggestions

Other holiday options exist, such as taking a holiday together – either at ordinary hotels or at facilities specifically geared for disabled or older people – or arranging a holiday for only your relative at one of the specialist providers, such as the John Grooms Association and Winged Fellowship.

If you choose to stay together at a hotel or holiday park, and feel you will need a short break from your relative but do not wish to leave them unsupervised, you may be able to book private home care assistance for them. Your local social services department should be able to help you access help in other areas. Alternatively, look in Yellow Pages in the particular area under 'Nursing Agencies' or 'Domestic Help' (there is currently no major section in Yellow Pages for home help agencies). Wherever in the UK you choose to holiday, ask the social services in that area about the availability of services you may need to use, such as Dial-A-Ride transport.

For more *information*

ⓘ Holidays for You and Me (address on p 122).

ⓘ John Grooms Association (address on p 123).

ⓘ Winged Fellowship (address on p 125).

Holiday ideas do not need to be boring!

If you are considering a break with the rest of your family and your older relative, you do not necessarily have to forsake all sense of adventure. Something such as a barge holiday could be ideal. The pace of life may help you unwind; it is not too hectic and is usually accessible to an older person; and if there are younger more active members of the family, the barge can be moored near towns or riverside pubs. If you need a short break from your relative, you can often walk a section of the tow-path while the boat sails on. Or you may opt for a caravan holiday for yourself and your relative, with younger family members camping on the same site nearby.

Remember that people with mild dementia may still derive great benefits from a holiday abroad.

Jo

'I find that it helps us to visit the same place every year. We always holidayed in France when I was younger, and taking my parents there, despite the fact they both suffer from dementia, brings back wonderful memories for all of us. It's amazing how much they remember when they get there. Travelling is not too much of a problem: it is only a day on the ferry and, with prior warning, the ferry company make sure we have help getting the wheelchair from the car and they reserve seats in the lounge for us.'

The emotional bonuses

If your relative is able to cope with going on holiday with you, even if just for a weekend, this can help sustain the relationship between you and increase social contact – facets of life that may become neglected because of other priorities such as maintaining the fabric of their home.

Rosa

'A weekend away together rekindled the affection and love I have for her.'

'I visit once a month at the weekend and the time just flies by, what with all the checks, shopping, letter writing and so on. Though I love Mother dearly, it takes its toll on my emotions. Because I'm working to tight deadlines, trying to fit everything into the visit, and because half of me is wondering how they are getting on at home, there are occasions when I "snap" at her for no good reason. We usually end up having some sort of disagreement. My husband suggested that I spend one of the weekends away with her – still minus the rest of the family. At first I thought it would be a waste of time that could have been better spent on jobs in her house. But it was brilliant. We went to the Lakes, and booked in at her favourite farmhouse B&B from years ago. We didn't really do much, but it didn't matter. It gave us the time to reminisce – and to just talk again to each other.'

Holidays without your relative

Having explored some options for holidaying with or near to your relative, you may decide that you need a holiday without them. There is no need to feel guilty about this: it is imperative that you do not neglect your own needs. Do not forget to leave contact numbers with your support network. Alternatively, while you are away you may prefer your relative to take a short stay in a care home: contact social services for a list of registered homes.

There is also a growing number of social service departments providing 'fostering' in carefully vetted family homes for those who do not wish to go into older people's homes for respite care. However, given the constraints on the budgets of social services, they may not fund such options if your relative seems to be coping at home. So make sure that either you yourself have budgeted for this or your relative has sufficient capital to purchase the services. The UKHCA have live-in carers – at a cost; but some form of paid support such as this is often the preferred option in some families who can afford it.

Checklist

Whatever holiday options you and your relative have chosen, if they are to be away from their own home for a while, do not forget to organise the type of practical steps you would take for your own household:

- cancel milk;
- cancel papers;
- mow lawn;
- inform neighbours/Neighbourhood Watch/support network;
- set timers on lights;
- check medication stocks if appropriate;
- check appliances not forgotten (such as hearing aids);
- cancel home help/day care/district nurse.

7 Dealing with your relative's finances

Like it or not, many care options have financial implications, and you may well find that you need to provide assistance with, or even take control of, your relative's financial affairs. This is an area that many carers find especially daunting and stressful, and is sometimes the aspect of care over which family members are most likely to squabble.

To protect a relative's interests it is important that reliable systems are set up, and this chapter will help you consider the ones most appropriate for your situation. It also highlights a concern so often initially ignored – the impact on your own finances of caring at a distance.

John

'I can cope with all the other aspects of caring, except the money.'

'I've never been the most organised of people when it comes to dealing with money. I am the kind of person who eventually gets round to paying the bills when the red reminder comes in. I always pay – eventually. Actually I've always had some difficulty in reading and understanding official letters and, because I'm nervous of them, I tend to ignore them until the last minute. But now that I have to look after my parents' finances because they both have mild dementia, I am sick with worry. I can't afford to let things slide, because if I don't pay a bill and a service is cut off the consequences will be far worse for them than for me. I went with them to see their bank manager and solicitor and it certainly helped, because they had a lot of useful suggestions for us.'

Caring at a distance costs ...

If you find that your relative needs help in dealing with their finances, it may be prudent to explain to them that you do not wish to pry into their affairs nor to take over: people usually have a right to keep their financial business totally private. The help they require may range from occasional support to almost total control set up within legal parameters, so your time commitment may vary enormously.

Preparatory steps

Even if your relative does not require assistance at the moment, time spent persuading them to keep all bills together in a file and to set up systems such as standing orders may pay dividends for you both at a later date.

If you can talk now about what finances might be available if the need for admission to a care home arises in the future, so much the better. If your relative owns their own property or has savings, liaising with an independent financial adviser about providing for care home fees later on would be a prudent move.

Try to get a clear picture of the situation at the outset. For example, it will help to know the pattern of expenditure on regular bills; if previous bills are not to hand, contact the offices of the companies concerned for help.

Clearing their debts

If you find that your relative has built up a considerable number of debts and you are now helping them with their finances, it may be prudent to obtain advice from the Citizens Advice Bureau. Alternatively, in some areas there are council-run money advice centres, or the organisation National Debtline can give advice (telephone number on p 123). Remember that the bills that must be dealt with first include mortgages, utilities and hire purchase.

Clearing the mortgage

One ongoing debt you may consider clearing is that of your relative's mortgage. However, if you do decide to encourage your relative to pay off their mortgage, it may be useful to investigate whether investing the same amount of money would give a high rate of interest and would therefore be more useful financially.

For more *i*nformation

❶ *Managing Other People's Money* published by Age Concern Books.

❶ Age Concern England Factsheet 22 *Legal arrangements for managing financial affairs.*

Financial help

Are they receiving all their entitlements?

Many people do not obtain the state benefits due to them – because of the bureaucratic processes, their lack of knowledge or the perceived 'stigma' at accepting them. You may have to stress to your relative that benefits are not charity handouts.

There are various grants and benefits available, from Income Support, Housing Benefit and free prescriptions to home improvement grants and help with the installation of a phone in some cases of severe hardship. Government help is available for energy-saving measures in the house: people over 60 years of age can apply for help under the Home Energy Efficiency Scheme. The Energy Saving Trust will also give free information and advice. (The phone numbers of these two schemes are on p 122.)

The local Benefits Agency office, Housing Department and Social Services Department are key ports of call to ascertain just what may be available to your relative. Care and Repair is an organisation that can also provide information on home improvement grants, Disability Alliance has information about benefits for people who are disabled, and the War Pensioners' Welfare Service may help if appropriate (see 'Useful addresses' on pp 119–126).

Do examine the various allowance criteria carefully. For example, Attendance Allowance can be claimed by someone who is ill or disabled, regardless of whether they have a carer providing a lot of support or if they have to manage alone. What matters is that they need help, not whether they are actually receiving it.

For more *i*nformation

𝒊   *Your Rights: A guide to money benefits for older people* published by Age Concern Books.

𝒊   DSS leaflet FB2 *Which Benefit?*.

𝒊   Carers National Association Information Sheet booklet *Benefits*.

𝒊   Age Concern England Factsheet 18 *A brief guide to money benefits*.

Other sources of help

Financial help for all sorts of matters may be available from a range of sources. For example, if your relative or their partner had at some time been employed by certain organisations such as the armed services or on the railways, or if they belong to particular social or religious groups, there may be financial assistance available from those organisations for housing, clothing, and so on.

> ### Leonora
>
> 'I was amazed to find that the department store where my uncle had worked all his life had a welfare department that followed up all their older ex-employees. Their representatives visit him annually and always ask if there are any "extras" he needs, and so far they have contributed towards some hand-made shoes he needed and a holiday.'

For more *i*nformation

i Social workers can help you identify and access these more diverse sources of help. .

i Charity Search may be able to help put you in touch with sources of financial help for older people (address on p 120).

Regular budgeting helps

We probably spend an hour or so a month paying our own bills, without having to allocate time to paying those of a relative. The best and easiest way of ensuring that regular payments are made – especially useful for maintaining utility services and therefore avoiding the risk of having services cut off – is by direct debit/standing order. If you are worried that your relative may cancel such an arrangement, you could arrange for the companies to send information to you as a nominated agent of the customer. Also, if your relative allows you to become a joint bank account holder, you will be kept informed by the bank of any alterations or problems. However, if your relative becomes mentally incapacitated the bank may terminate this arrangement.

Some older people are unconvinced about the merits of such modern cash transfer schemes. A joint visit to the bank manager may help, as we often listen to the advice of others rather than our own family. Alternatively, your relative may find it helpful to budget for things such as telephone bills and television licence by buying the relevant savings stamps. (It is worth bearing in mind, though, that they cannot be replaced if they are lost or stolen.) If they choose to pay regular bills by cash in person, you may need to make some regular checks of the receipts. A side benefit to your relative paying bills in person, though, is that they are making a regular trip out.

If your relative needs help with the collection of their state benefits, you may wish to consider one of the following.

Acting as an agent

If your relative's income is from state benefits only, and if they do not have assets such as a house, you could act as your relative's agent and collect their pension. Your relative will need to sign the front of each order and to complete Part 1 on the back, and you will have to sign Part 2. If this is a long-term arrangement, you can obtain an identification card from your local Benefits Agency or complete the form in leaflet AP1, *Helping Hand: how you help friends and relatives with physical disabilities claim the Social Security due to them.*

Acting as an appointee

If your relative is no longer able to manage their money, you may need to become an appointee. The conditions are similar to those for an agent, in that your relative should not have assets and is dependent on state benefits. Leaflet AP1, mentioned above, includes an application form. The Benefits Agency will check that:

■ your relative is indeed unable to manage their own affairs;
■ you are the right person to take over and that you will use the money for your relative's well-being;
■ you fully understand your responsibilities.

As an appointee you have the right to claim, collect and spend the benefits on behalf of your relative.

Steps to take in your relative's mental disorder

Another aspect of the issue of finances occurs when the older person cannot manage their own affairs because of mental disorder. This can present enormous worries to others. However, there are routes that can be taken, including obtaining an Enduring Power of Attorney. An ordinary Power of Attorney allows you access to your relative's accounts but is invalidated if the person becomes mentally incapable of understanding their affairs. An Enduring Power of Attorney, like an ordinary Power of Attorney, must be arranged in advance of mental confusion, but continues afterwards, once it is registered by the Public Trust Office.

It is strongly recommended that you obtain legal advice from a solicitor or the Citizens Advice Bureau if you plan to pursue this route. Nevertheless, if your relative does create an Enduring Power of Attorney, it can help enormously in relieving a later stressful situation. It is worth remembering that, under an Enduring Power of Attorney agreement, you have only limited powers to make gifts to yourself or others out of the donor's estate – for example, in line with what the donor might have been expected to do, such as to reimburse your travel expenses on their behalf or to buy a birthday present for a grandchild.

For more *information*

𝑖 Contact the Public Trust Office (address on p 124).

Court of Protection

If your relative becomes confused without having given you an Enduring Power of Attorney, you may apply for help from the Court of Protection. Under the Court of Protection Rules and the Mental Health Act 1983, a 'receiver' can be appointed (usually a relative, solicitor, neighbour or friend), who can have authority to do anything that the person would do if they were capable. It is worth noting that many of the costs involved come out of the person's assets, not the receiver's, but spending is tightly controlled; the receiver is expected to make at least one annual visit to the person and to file annual accounts of their dealings with the person's affairs, and to pay an annual fee.

Applications are made to the Court of Protection in England and Wales, or the Office of Care and Protection in Northern Ireland (addresses on pp 121 and 124). Different rules apply in Scotland (see below).

Even if the matter of an Enduring Power of Attorney has not yet arisen, perhaps the best thing you could do would be to arrange a joint appointment now with the family solicitor and your relative's bank manager so that they know how you may be dealing with affairs in the future.

For more *i*nformation

ℹ Age Concern England Factsheet 22 *Legal arrangements for managing financial affairs.*

Managing someone's affairs in Scotland

A legal principle (called *negotiorum gestio*) allows you to act on behalf of someone who is mentally incapable, provided your actions are for their benefit. The principle assumes that the person would have authorised you if they *had* been capable, so it may be useful in an emergency – for example, immediate repairs are needed to your relative's home and you need to claim back the money you spend on their behalf. Some organisations may not accept this informal arrangement.

Power of Attorney

If the Power of Attorney was signed after 1 January 1991, it will remain valid if the person who gave it becomes mentally incapable. A solicitor must prepare the Power of Attorney.

Curator bonis

If your relative has not given a Power of Attorney and is mentally incapable of looking after their affairs or of appointing someone to do this, a *curator bonis* may be needed. This is an individual appointed by and responsible to the Court. Usually – but not necessarily – a solicitor or accountant is appointed, and they must manage all the financial affairs and property of the person.

The application to the Court for a curator bonis to be appointed is prepared by a solicitor, usually on behalf of a close relative of the person. Having a curator bonis appointed is expensive, and any professional will charge an annual administration fee. It is therefore not recommended for people with capital of less than £15,000.

For more *i*nformation

ℹ️ *Dementia: Money and Legal Matters* – available (free to carer) from Alzheimer Scotland – Action on Dementia (address on p 119).

ℹ️ Age Concern Scotland Factsheet 22 *Legal arrangements for managing financial affairs.*

ℹ️ *Information for families of persons subject to curatory* – free leaflet from The Accountant of Court (address on p 119).

Making a Will

A very difficult financial situation for a family to deal with can be when a relative dies intestate: that is to say, without having left a Will. Family members can end up in dispute over what the relative had intended by way of distributing their assets, and an acrimonious situation may develop.

It can be hard to broach the subject of making a Will, but is reassuring to all concerned once completed. It would be wise to encourage your relative, if they are 'of sound mind', to receive independent advice from a solicitor, accessing legal aid if appropriate. Alternatively, DIY Will forms are available from large stationers and from some charities.

Kirsty-Jane

'I have heard cynics say, "Where there's a Will there's a relative". But it is so important to get these kinds of things sorted out before the time comes. My brother was not very happy about me persuading Dad to make a Will, even though I made sure I distanced myself from the preparation of the Will and used a solicitor. He realised afterwards that it had saved an awful lot of time and acrimony in sorting out the affairs, which was important to both of us as we lived at the other end of the country from Dad.'

Note **If your relative does make a Will, make sure you know where a copy is held.**

For more *i*nformation

- **𝒊** Age Concern England Factsheet 7 *Making your Will.*
- **𝒊** Age Concern England Factsheet 14 *Probate: Dealing with someone's estate.*

The impact on your own finances

There is, unfortunately, no doubt about it. Caring from a distance will cost you money. How you feel about that or indeed manage it depends entirely on your own personal circumstances; however, a few aspects are discussed here.

Agnes

'Mum likes me to do bits and pieces of her housework at night when I call in after work to see her, and I don't mind at all. She says she doesn't want a stranger doing it. But for every extra task you take on, something in your own life has to go, so it means I have to budget to pay for a cleaner to help me in my house.'

Travel costs

If you find that you need to travel a long distance to visit your relative, do not under-estimate what this will cost. It is worth checking out the discount times and rates on trains and coaches, and booking trips well in advance, as these tend to be cheaper than last-minute bookings or travelling at peak times. Other offers that may help include family travel offers and season tickets; and look out for special fare promotions, for example in the supermarkets.

If you travel by car, you must budget for more petrol and maintenance costs. A cheap run-around car may be fine locally, but driving takes on a more daunting dimension when the car is expected to transport you hundreds of miles several times a year. Joining a national recovery service may not then be a luxury but a necessity: the last thing you need is the added stress of being stranded without help.

With modern technology becoming ever easier and cheaper, you may think it worthwhile to invest in a mobile phone so that your relative can always get in touch. Check out the limited use and special offers available – but bear in mind the long-term cost to you of monthly rental and advance notification of termination of contract clauses.

If you are caring from a shorter distance and visiting quite frequently, you may find that you are doing 'bits and pieces' of shopping for your relative, and not asking for or taking reimbursement. This is fine, as long as you can genuinely afford it, but these small amounts of money can soon mount up and create extra pressure on you. Or you may find that you buy 'thank you' presents for support network contacts. However minor the expenditure, do not neglect these smaller amounts in the overview of your own finances.

8 Keeping in touch

Regular contact with your relative is vital, although how frequent this is needs to be balanced with emotional and financial considerations. You will no doubt want to check periodically that everything is well, but you may find phone calls difficult or even at times distressing. It is usually easier to check up on things face-to-face, and not being able to do this can be one of the most frustrating aspects of caring at a distance.

In the first part of this chapter we look at ways of maintaining contact – and of minimising the expense. The second part briefly examines the implications of caring and keeping in touch at a greater distance, that is to say abroad.

Remember that you may be keeping in touch not only with an older relative but also with a primary carer (see Chapter 9, 'You as a secondary carer'). Staying in touch may be a lifeline for them.

Winston

'My sister tells everyone she keeps in touch regularly with Dad.'

'I don't know who she is trying to convince – the rest of the family or herself. After all, "regular" could be once every hundred years! And in her case, it's only once a year on Christmas Day. We all live hundreds of miles away from him, so we all incur costs when we phone, but the rest of us take it in turns: we have a rota. I know she hasn't got as much spare cash as some of the others, and she probably never really got on with him, but it needn't be a long call. Just to hear her voice and know she is thinking about him is enough for Dad. Mind you, I think part of the trouble is actually because she leaves it so long between calls: the less often you phone, the less there is to say because you lose the thread of communication, and end up with those long silences you try desperately to fill. Anyway I've suggested to her that she write to him instead.'

Working out what you can do

There are, of course, no definitive answers to the questions of how often or how best to make contact with your relative if they live some distance away. You will probably find that a pattern of contact emerges, perhaps a phone call every other day, once a week, a letter every month ...

However, how do you balance the need to keep in touch with very real financial implications? The telephone is a wonderful piece of technology but you may not think so when you receive the bill!

Telephone

Telephone discount schemes

First, do not forget the advantages of discount schemes with both British Telecom (BT) and other service providers such as Cable & Wireless. With some non-BT providers you may have to remember to use a special button or code number on your BT telephone, or to have a specific line installed.

Currently BT operate a 'Friends and Family' scheme with discounted numbers. The major phone companies compete aggressively with each other and it is well worth keeping abreast of their current rates. Either way, remember that discounts *are* available, that their competitive rates vary, and most companies can be contacted free of charge (BT on 0800 800 150, and Cable & Wireless on 0500 500 196).

Another point to remember is that, if you are the one who makes all the phone calls and your relative rarely uses the telephone, they may be eligible for a limited user discount from BT. Again, ring their customer helpline for free information.

If there is little money to spare, a very effective cheap way of keeping in touch daily is to arrange to telephone each other at a certain time – either the same every day or different according to the plan. You dial their number, let it ring three times (or whatever number you choose) and hang up; your relative then dials your number, lets it ring three times and hangs up. Although the phone companies might object to this loss of income for them, this is a good way to ask and answer that everything is all right. The arrangement is worked so that, if either person doesn't ring, suitable pre-agreed emergency procedures are put in place.

Dealing with telephone problems

It may happen that, while you are on the phone, your relative goes off to check something, such as food cooking or their diary, and forgets that you are on the other end, or they fail to replace the receiver correctly. This can be very distressing, as well as inconvenient to you, as it means that you cannot use the phone to contact anyone else while you are still connected (if they rang you). If you fail to attract their attention by shouting or blowing a whistle, you need to go to another phone and ask the operator to help. They will transmit an ear-piercing tone down the line to attract attention. If this fails, your only other courses of action are to use another phone to ring a friendly neighbour and ask them to pop round to your relative, or to wait until your relative notices that the phone is off the hook or, eventually, to ask the police to call in and check if you fear the worst. A local contact who will call in and check that everything is all right is invaluable in these circumstances, as well as when the phone is unanswered or there is a continual engaged tone; otherwise you may have to resign yourself to a night of worry.

Debbie

'She said she was going to answer the door, and she never came back to the phone.'

'I shouted down the phone, blew a whistle, banged a saucepan – all sorts, but Mum's hard of hearing. I put the receiver down thinking that she would eventually replace hers, but every time I checked we were still connected. I went out to a phone box and called the operator who sent a really loud signal to her phone, but still to no avail. It was quite late at night and I was worried sick that when she had answered the door perhaps someone had attacked her. Your mind runs riot in these circumstances. So I telephoned her neighbour from the call box and, bless her, she got out of bed and went round to Mum's. She discovered that Mum had ostensibly put the phone on its receiver (she must have forgotten that I was on the other end). But it had a coiled cord which had become so tangled that it was easy to think you had put the phone back properly when you hadn't. She went out and got Mum a phone with a straight cable the next day, and I sent her the money.'

Note If the cost of installing a telephone is a problem for your relative, help may be available. Contact social services for details.

Emergency numbers

One of the most practical steps you can take is to print a large notice beside your relative's phone with emergency contact numbers – the fewer the better. Include the 999 emergency number, as in a panic this may be forgotten. Remember to write in lower case letters if your relative is suffering from dementia.

Mobile phones

Another aspect of keeping in touch is that of being contactable in emergencies. This is where a mobile phone may be useful, although you may decide that it makes you too accessible, if you have a relative who constantly telephones you.

Craig

'I made sure Auntie's neighbours, doctor and the home help had my mobile number. But I have to confess I never told her I had a mobile; otherwise she would never have been off the phone. As it was, I used to have to keep my answerphone switched on because she would phone roughly every two hours, day in and day out.'

Phone gifts

A telephone can be an ideal present for your relative. You could buy one that is compatible with hearing aids, or has an exceptionally loud ring, or includes a flashing light, or has a large or illuminated key pad, or indeed an extra phone for the bedroom for security. Telephone stamps towards the payment of bills also make welcome gifts.

Letter writing

Obviously the phone is not the only means of contact, and older people in particular often appreciate receiving a letter. You may decide to make letter writing an important part of your strategy for maintaining communication, as a substitute for, or supplement to, telephoning.

Letters are also very useful as a confirmation of or follow-up to any arrangements made with your relative, either face-to-face or by telephone. It need not take an obvious form, but can be incorporated discreetly in phrases such as, 'I know we talked about what we will do at Easter. I'm looking forward to seeing you on the 16th. Don't worry, I'll ring you on that day when I am about to leave home.'

Letter writing is also a useful way of confirming for your relative what arrangements you may have made with organisations or tradespeople on their behalf.

101

Do not always expect a reply to your letters: it does not mean that they are any less valued or welcomed. You may like to give your relative a gift of a set of notelets with already stamped and addressed envelopes, to encourage them to write to you or other family members.

You may also be able to help your relative to keep in touch with others, particularly at times such as Christmas. If your relative doesn't find writing very easy, you could write and address their cards for them. If they are unable to sign all the cards, perhaps you could photocopy their signature and stick it inside each card. At various times throughout the year you may be able to help them by typing and copying a 'round robin' letter for family and friends. If you have access to a computer, you could set up a label address file so that address labels could be printed off.

Other ways of keeping in touch

As well as letter writing and telephoning, you might consider using audio cassettes (spoken letters), home videos and photographs.

Try to involve your relative by asking them to record their own messages. Or they could record the games they played as a child or growing up during the war or what the 1960s were like, and so on. These sorts of exercises can be particularly useful if young children or grandchildren are involved, who might be doing school projects on these subjects, but they are also about communication and keeping in touch being a two-way thing. Asking your relative's advice is also helpful (make up a query if necessary), such as their jam recipe or what was the name of someone you both knew years ago.

Technological advances in communication

Whilst much of this book tends to focus on caring at a distance for people with physical or mental impairment, of course your older relative may be extremely able and active. If this is the case, do not ignore the possibilities that technological advances bring about. The following two carers at a distance are by no means typical of the masses, but do show an imaginative approach to keeping in touch.

Jordan

'I work from home and have a fax machine. It dawned on me that I could communicate with Pop, who lives in the States, instantly, if he had one too. The prices of them have come down over the years and they are more affordable for many. It's brilliant – I wish I had thought of this before.'

Rachael

'Mum is amazingly active for her 73 years, and likes to keep up with what the grandchildren do. So when they kept on about the Internet she decided to blow some of her savings, buy a computer, and join them. She went to classes at college, where she raised a few eyebrows! But she loves her new hobby, and I don't worry about her so much – because even though she is brilliant for her age you still worry don't you, when they are far away. She regularly uses 'the Net' to get in touch with us, and has a great new hobby. Wonderful really: I would never have thought of it myself.'

Caring at a greater distance

So far, we have looked at caring at a distance with the focus on living apart but in the same country. Increasingly, though, families are having to cope with caring from further afield. If the younger members of the family have emigrated, the sources of advice and help in the book so far would be applicable. However, what if the older person is the one living abroad? How do you keep in touch with their needs and the help available?

Much of the practical advice is still valid whatever country you are visiting, but extra effort may have to be made to discover how to access help.

The consulates or embassies of nations vary enormously in the amount of information they will give you about sources of potential help in their own countries, but it is still well worth contacting them at the outset. Telephone numbers are available from Directory Enquiries, or often from travel agents. It is worth remembering that many nations may only provide some types of specialist care to those who have lived in the country for a qualifying period, contributed to their economy, have private insurance cover, or indeed have become citizens of that country. Perhaps the soundest advice to be given is that, if you have a relative who has retired to another land, it is imperative to make enquiries about care before it is needed – and to double-check their insurance cover. It would also be useful to ascertain whether your relative wishes to return to Britain in the event of, say, the onset of dementia: in effect, an advance directive.

Phil

'Mum and Dad emigrated to Spain and thoroughly enjoyed their retirement. They lived in an area where there weren't many other ex-pats, and learned to speak fluent Spanish. When Dad developed dementia they were able to access help and support. However, he reverted to his mother tongue of English, which caused extra frustration for him in communicating with people. My parents had already talked a bit about what to do if one of them had a problem, so Mum sold up their villa and they returned home. She was really sad about making the decision, but felt it was for the best.'

If you yourself have emigrated to the UK, you may be worried about your older relatives still living in your native country and would like to bring them here so that you may care for them. Do bear in mind that UK immigration laws are extremely strict, that visa applications can take a long time, and that your relative's being given permission to reside here depends on many circumstances, including your financial ability to support them. Sue Ward's _Ethnic Elders' Benefits Handbook_ (published by Age Concern Books) has a lot of information that you might find helpful.

Ryuichi

'I have lived in England for many years but never really given a thought to what would happen when my father became older and frailer: it's the kind of thing you push to the back of your mind. I wish I had planned for this earlier, because now neither of us would want to leave our respective countries.'

Care in other countries

Provision for older people across the globe is so diverse that it would take a separate book to cover. If your relative is thinking of living abroad, it is sensible to find out first what services are available in the chosen country. An initial enquiry could be made to that country's embassy or consulate in the UK.

If someone has lived and worked in the UK, paying into the state benefits system, and then decides to emigrate, some UK benefit entitlements may be 'exported'. To find out what applies in your relative's case, contact the local Benefits Agency.

Note **If you need to send money to your relative abroad, banks have various schemes for the transfer of funds to a bank near them. There is also a new Post Office 'Moneygram' facility whereby money can be transferred world-wide in minutes.**

For more *i*nformation

- *Ethnic Elders' Benefits Handbook* published by Age Concern Books.

- Local Post Offices can supply a leaflet about Moneygrams, or telephone freephone 0800 897 198.

9 You as a secondary carer

So far, the book has focused on you as the only or primary carer, caring at a distance. However, it may be the case that another of your relations is actually nearer to your older relative and is the primary carer, with you in a support role. How best can you provide that support? Will it be required or indeed welcomed? You may have to deal with a wide range of emotions, from gratitude for your help to resentment of your help or that you do not do more.

The following section explores ways in which you can provide assistance, no matter how distant you are. Being a secondary carer can be an invaluable role, and there are many people in families who can make a contribution in supporting the closer carer.

Elder abuse is an almost taboo subject in our society, and hopefully you will never have to deal with it. However, if you do, the second part of this chapter should help you cope positively.

Maria

'I resent how everyone feels about my sister's visits.'

'I make a round trip of almost 500 miles every month without fail to visit Dad. It's tiring, my own family miss out on my time and energy, and to be quite honest I can barely afford the petrol. No one even comments about it. It's not that I want everyone congratulating or thanking me, it's just that it is in such contrast to my sister's visits.

'She comes twice a year from the States, and everyone – Dad, his sister, all the neighbours – make a big thing about it ... how wonderful it is that she comes all this way ... how exhausting it must be. But she works for the airline and doesn't even have to pay for her trips, for heaven's sake. She calls in on her way back from her work trip to Paris or wherever, so there's actually no extra time commitment – and it doesn't cost her a penny!

'When she visits, Dad takes her out for a slap-up meal to celebrate. When I am there it's taken for granted that I'll cook. She was always the favourite, I suppose. When Mum was alive she always reminded him of how I am the one who took on the burden of looking out for them.

'To be fair, when my sister does visit, she always asks what she can do to help. But if she thinks that offering to hoover twice a year is the best help, then she is mistaken. I know she has enough money to afford to buy Dad a few luxuries, but I don't feel comfortable in asking her to do that, so I suppose as long as I don't say anything then things won't change. If only she would just ask what he needs.'

The comments above are very like the situation in which people are played off against each other. This can happen, for example, if your relative is very critical of the primary carer when you call or visit; or never seems as ill when you visit; or claims that the primary carer is (or is not) doing things, which the primary carer says isn't true. It can be extremely important not to 'take sides' but to check things out first in a non-confrontational way.

Being there for them

There is no doubt that many primary carers will welcome – and need – an extra source of help. This could be as simple as a supportive phone call and/or letter every now and then: the key factor is to stay in touch.

If you are not in a position to visit and help, or this is only a rare occasion, are you able to provide financial help? Do offer this to your relative and the primary carer: they may not feel able to ask for your help. The help could be in the form of regular cheques, or always paying certain bills, paying for holidays or regular 'treats' such as a trip to the theatre for the carer and/or relative, or home improvements, to give but a few suggestions.

Always remember that, even if you experience a reaction from the carer such as anger or resentment, it does not necessarily mean that your offer of help is any less needed, and you will have to work through this.

Be aware of the impact that your occasional visits may have, not only on your relative but also on the primary carer. If necessary, remind others of the invaluable support that the primary carer is giving: this may be the only acknowledgement of their caring.

Adopt a positive attitude for the primary carer, and be careful not to criticise. You may feel that you would do things differently, but it's easy to judge situations at a distance and you may not be in possession of all the facts. Besides, if the carer is coping with the situation, is change really necessary?

Practical help on your visits

Try to find out what gaps may exist in the caring: ask the primary carer. You may find that you are in a position to view the situation more objectively than the primary carer, and you may therefore be able to help access services and information, or to do some of the forward planning that might help in any future crisis. You may have more time, or be more able/better placed, to write letters or complete forms. On your visits, try to carry out tasks the carer finds difficult or dislikes, such as mowing the lawn or dusting. Or cook some meals to put in the freezer. Or, if they enjoy doing a certain type of thing but simply have not had the time, you could look after the older person to give them that time. Some visitors assume that the carer will automatically want to go out and therefore only ever offer to look after the older person within the home environment. Ask the carer what they would like: you may find that they would prefer you to go out with the older person so that they can have some precious time alone in the house.

If you visit to give the primary carer a break, it would be prudent to discuss with them any practical help that you intend to offer. Otherwise it may be misconstrued, as one cousin in a family found out when she thought she was helping by clearing out a bedroom:

Sandra

'My cousin told everyone that we had crawled out of the woodwork and cleared the place out.'

'Last time we stayed for the weekend my aunt asked me to sort out the spare bedroom. I was delighted to be able to help and thought her daughter would be pleased, but a week afterwards I had the police at my door about a theft. There was nothing of any value in that room, I swear – only dusty newspapers from the year dot and some broken trinket boxes, and I left everything at their house for the rubbish collection. But my aunt, who has dementia, accused me of stealing some jewellery (which they later found), and my cousin said I had thrown away things with great sentimental value. It's all blown over now but it could have become really nasty. I understood when my cousin was initially huffed about my help – as she said, my aunt had always refused to let her touch the room! And I suppose at the time they genuinely thought the jewellery was missing. If I were a different type of person I would probably never visit again. But I know I'm the only one they've got so I couldn't do that, although I'll be more careful in future.'

Who is the primary/secondary carer?

Niamh

'I have two brothers who live nearer than I do, but I am expected to be the principal carer even though I have to cross the sea to get to her.'

109

'My two brothers actually live in my homeland and are nearer my mother. However, she seems to save up all her problems for my visits, purely on the basis that I am her only daughter and a nurse to boot. She says things like, "Why should I have home help when I have you?" and "Sons shouldn't be expected to help in the same way". Yet I live hundreds of miles away. The strain of knowing that she waits for my visits really spoils them – these visits use up my holidays from work – and my brothers don't recognise that fact.'

Niamh's experiences illustrate that the primary/secondary carer role in any family situation is not always immediately identifiable to the outsider, and anyone planning to offer support to a more frequent carer may have to examine the situation closely to identify who may benefit from their practical or emotional support. It is also arguable that even now, in this emancipated age, the primary carer is often female – even if her personal circumstances are the least conducive to a successful caring role. The life-long expectations of a relative, for example of 'traditional' male/female roles, may well affect your caring relationship and the attitudes of other family members.

Elder abuse

The issue of elder abuse is almost taboo in our society, and not widely discussed. Yet in the Homer 1990 survey – part of a paper published for the *British Medical Journal* (A Homer & C Gilleard, 15 December 1990), which looked at the abuse of elders by carers – 45 per cent of carers interviewed admitted to some form of abuse, and 20 per cent indicated that the abuse had been physical and/or verbal. Most people immediately think of physical abuse, not verbal abuse and neglect, but abuse can take the form of deprivation of things such as food and the company of others, misuse of medication or money, sexual abuse, or psychological abuse.

It is not always easy to see the signs immediately, and it can be even harder to admit to yourself, in the first instance, that abuse may be occurring. However, ignoring the situation will help no one in the long run. Abuse is a criminal offence, and the abuser needs help, with a supportive, non-judgmental approach. Remember that people under great stress can act in a way that is totally out of character.

What should you do if you suspect abuse?

It must be stressed that one must not jump to conclusions too readily without investigation but, equally, abuse should never be ignored. The older person needs help – and so does the abuser.

You may choose to speak to your relative alone to try to ascertain some facts. You may then decide to tell the primary carer about your concerns. Be sure to offer your help and support. Whatever you choose to do, though, you must inform social services of your concerns – a social worker can be invaluable in ascertaining the facts and advising on sources of help. They will take everybody's needs into consideration.

Jason

'I suppose I knew my sister was at the end of her tether, but I didn't think she would ever harm Dad.'

'It's just not in her nature to harm anybody, so when I eventually discovered that the bruising was not accidental, I just couldn't believe it. Looking back, I suppose the signs of emotional strain were there. Maybe I chose to ignore them – and maybe I simply did not give enough emotional support. The best thing I did was to get professional help for my sister. I didn't find it easy suggesting that she might be hitting him, but it had to be said. Anyway with the help of the social worker and the GP the situation is much better now, with respite care arranged for Dad regularly.'

What signs should you look out for?

Apart from any obvious signs that your relative is not being well cared for, for example not washed or unkempt, there may be

111

unexplained falls, bruising, burns in unusual places, excessive alcohol or medication consumption (by the carer or the older person themselves), bruising from finger pressure, consistent hunger, frequent soiled clothing, unattended pressure sores or urine burns. Signs of sexual abuse include pain, bruising, bleeding or itching in the genital areas, or the victim may suddenly resist toileting. Look out also for signs of restraint – not only the obvious ones of being tied in chairs, but others such as the older person being kept in a reclining chair and unable to get out, or furniture arranged to impede movement.

If abused, the older person may be agitated, depressed, constantly fatigued, overly subservient or anxious. The carer may be displaying a variety of emotions from anger, frustration, despair, anxiety and worry, to resentment. If they admit to some of these feelings, they may well blame them on another – real or fictitious – scenario.

Remember that abuse could be occurring in reverse – the older person may, perhaps owing to dementia, be abusing the carer, who in turn tries to cover up or deny it.

Unintentional neglect

There may be unintentional neglect rather than wilful abuse, such as withholding drinks to alleviate incontinence without realising the dangers of dehydration, or not attending to the loss of essential aids such as spectacles.

From your point of view

Hopefully you will never have to deal with this situation but, if you do, remember that it may compound any feelings of guilt you may already have about the frequency of your visits or the amount of support you are able to offer. Whatever level of help you have felt able to give, you will need to reappraise the situation from your own point of view and see if you can possibly offer any more support – financial, emotional or practical. The carer needs to know that they are important as well as the older person.

For more *i*nformation

i Speak to a social worker, GP or counsellor.

i Put the primary carer in touch with the above.

i Put the primary carer in touch with an association such as the Relaxation for Living Trust (number and address on p 124) or the Samaritans (number in the telephone directory).

i Contact Action on Elder Abuse (number and address on p 119).

10 Practical purchases to make life easier

As anyone with an older person for whom they buy gifts knows, it can be very difficult to choose something that will be useful or used! When you are caring at a distance, gifts may take on additional importance. As one carer said, 'Because I can't visit frequently, I feel the need to buy really good presents to make up for it.'

The purpose of this chapter is to provide practical suggestions to suit every taste, circumstance and budget. With careful thought you can buy gifts that not only may be welcomed by the recipient but will also make life easier for you on your visits, or may provide additional peace of mind for you at a distance by improving your relative's safety or comfort.

Nancy

'What do you buy the grandmother who always says she has everything she needs?'

'You know that things like bubble bath and scarves will just get put away in a cupboard or given to someone else! A few years ago I decided to buy her things that I knew would help me to help her. Sometimes she doesn't really appreciate them at first, but more often than not, months later, she will say something like, "That gadget you bought me has been a godsend".

114

Even if she doesn't comment, it makes me feel better to know I've helped her safety or health or independence in some way, and I have to confess that many of the gifts have made life easier for me when I'm helping her on my visits. Mind you, one of the most unusual gifts, and one she loved, was a mushroom-growing kit for indoors. She can no longer cope with gardening, which she used to adore, but got great satisfaction from still growing something to eat and it was really simple to use.'

What can you buy?

What do you buy the person who seems to have accumulated everything over the years? It's a hard enough decision if you live nearby, but even worse if you have to send the gift by post.

Your choice may not be imaginative, but can be the easiest solution – and you don't need to create any extra stress for yourself. Send flowers or a plant by post (Interflora, Teleflorist, and the Post Office can all help and their numbers are in the local directory). Almost every hobby has its own society, which may be able to provide postal gifts or suggestions, such as the philatelic society or theatrical societies. It is also worth remembering that you can send luxury foodstuffs such as smoked salmon through the post, which could provide a welcome treat. Or a year's subscription to a favourite magazine will mean that every week or month there is something to look forward to.

If you feel that it is more important to address basic food needs, a present you could provide year after year is a basket filled with tinned foods, which you make up by buying something for it every week, and deliver to your relative personally. Or arrange to buy a hamper and have it sent: most of the national catalogue companies provide this service.

Browse through catalogues

The type of catalogue that sometimes arrives tucked inside magazines or newspapers and contains unusual gifts is well worth a look, as many of the items can be very useful for an older person. Examples include handwarmers automatically activated by touch or heated in a microwave; thermal socks and gloves; non-slip soles for shoes; fleecy underblankets; infra-red pain relievers; magnifiers for pages; and lights that automatically come on in wardrobes and cupboards.

Gardening gifts

Considering gardening gifts gives you great scope, and can certainly prove advantageous to your own situation in saving you time on your visits. Probably one of the most practical gifts you can buy to help with garden maintenance is bark chippings. (Do you really have time to do the weeding?) It is invaluable for providing ground cover that requires next to no maintenance. Gravel rather than grass for paths has two advantages: it needs no mowing and, being noisy to walk on, is thus a deterrent to burglars. A disadvantage is that it might be more painful if your relative were to fall on it.

Is it possible to replace all the grass with paving or gravel? This may not be the kind of garden that would appeal to you at your own home but it is certainly to be considered if the maintenance of the garden falls to you, and an attractive appearance can still be obtained, especially if you site a few tubs of a low maintenance shrub such as a conifer. If you are buying some shrubs as a gift, thorny ones such as juniper, holly and pyracantha planted underneath windows will help home security. If replacing the grass is not an option, you might pay for the lawn to be cut every two weeks or so during the summer.

Forget planting annuals: you are going to need to devote your valuable time to other things – but if you really want a splash of colour, buy nasturtium seeds – they thrive on neglect and produce more flowers the poorer the soil. Let Nature have its way and do not bother thinning out to save precious time.

If your relative still enjoys gardening, practical gifts you can buy include specialised gardening tools such as a 'weedkey' which allows them to remove weeds easily without stooping; it can also be used from a wheelchair. A 'hover' type of lawnmower is fairly light and easy to manoeuvre, and an electric edge trimmer is another useful aid, whether it is your relative or you who is looking after the grass. (Remember, of course, to use a residual current device (RCD).) Other ideas include outdoor lights to run parallel with a path (solar-powered ones illuminate automatically at dusk), a kneeler stool, or a gardening service to help with the maintenance. (Consult Yellow Pages, Talking Pages, or any of the local garden centres for a gardening service; for the others, any good gardening catalogue or one of the gift catalogues will probably help.)

Gift suggestions

With the other pressures of caring at a distance, you may not have a lot of time to devote to thinking about presents. The following is an alphabetical list of possibilities compiled from the experience of many carers at a distance. You will find that a number of the suggestions listed here are described elsewhere in this book as part of helping you care at a distance successfully:

- AA or RAC cover if still driving
- Automatic lights that switch on at dusk
- Blankets
- Can opener (electric, Magican-type or wall-mounted)
- Cordless kettle
- Deep-fat fryer (electric)
- Door viewer (spy-hole)
- Fire blanket/extinguisher
- Flask
- Foot spa
- Gardening tools
- Hairdresser – visits to or by

- Aromatherapy/massage
- Ashtrays (deep and heavy)
- Back rest
- Bark chippings
- Burglar alarm
- Carbon monoxide alarms/detectors
- Cordless iron
- Day care at a centre or residential home
- Door chain
- Dosette-type medication dispenser
- Flowers
- Gardening service
- Gravel
- Hamper of food
- Home-help service

117

- Illuminated light switch surround
- Laundry service
- Lumbar support cushion
- Microwave
- Non-slip flooring
- Non-slip tray
- Page magnifier
- Pet insurance
- Postal gift services
- Security lights
- Security marker pens
- Stamps to pay electricity, etc
- Tea-maker
- Telephone or related equipment
- Television licence paid
- Thermometers – house, fridge, freezer
- Underblanket

- Infra-red pain reliever
- Infra-red sensor lights
- Long-life light bulbs
- Magazine subscription
- Mushroom-growing kit
- Non-slip spray for shoe soles
- Personal alarm
- Plugs with handles
- Residual current device (RCD)
- Smoke alarms
- Subscription connected with a hobby
- Telephone bill paid/ phone stamps
- Thermal clothing
- Timer switch for lights
- Travel rugs
- Window locks

Useful addresses

Accountant of Court
Information about curator bonis in Scotland

Parliament House
Parliament Square
Edinburgh EH1 1RQ
Tel: 0131-225 2595

Action on Elder Abuse
Aims to prevent abuse of older people by raising awareness, education, promoting research and the collection and dissemination of information

Astral House
1268 London Road
London SW16 4ER
Tel: 0181-679 2648
Elder Abuse Response:
0800 7314141
10am–4.30pm weekdays

Age Concern England

see p 127

Alzheimer Scotland – Action on Dementia
Supports a network of carers' support groups

22 Drumsheugh Gardens
Edinburgh EH3 7RN
Tel: 0800 317 817
24-hour helpline:
0131-220 6155
Admin: 0131-243 1453

Alzheimer's Disease Society
Information and support for people caring for someone with dementia

Gordon House
10 Greencoat Place
London SW1P 1PH
Tel: 0171-306 0606

Benefits Agency (part of the DSS)

Freephone line no longer
exists; refer to local office:
number in telephone
directory

British Association for Counselling
To find out about counselling services in your area

1 Regent Place
Rugby
Warwickshire CV21 2PJ
Tel: 01788 578328

British Red Cross
Provides home aids, advice and support

9 Grosvenor Crescent
London SW1X 7EJ
Tel: 0171-235 5454

Care and Repair
Advice on home improvements and grants

Castle House
Kirtley Drive
Nottingham NG7 1LD
Tel: 0115-979 9091

Carers National Association
Advice and support for carers

20–25 Glasshouse Yard
London EC1A 4JS
Adviceline:
0171-490 8898
(10–12, 2–4 weekdays)
Tel: 0171-490 8818

Charity Search
Information about possible sources of financial help for older people

25 Portview Road
Avonmouth
Bristol BS11 9LD
Tel: 0117-982 4060

Cinnamon Trust
Information and support in care for pets

Foundry House
Foundry Square
Hayle
Cornwall TR27 4HH
Tel: 01736 757900

Citizens Advice Bureau
Advice on legal, financial and consumer matters. Good general source of information

Address in local telephone directory

Contact the Elderly
Provides companions for housebound people

15 Henrietta Street
London WC2E 8QH
Tel: 0171-240 0630

Continence Foundation
Advice and information about incontinence problems

The Basement
2 Doughty Street
London WC1N 2PH
Tel: 0171-404 6875

120

Counsel and Care
Advice on remaining at home,
or about care homes

Lower Ground Floor
Twyman House
16 Bonny Street
London NW1 9PG
Tel: 0171-485 1550

Court of Protection
If you need to take over the affairs
of someone who is mentally incapable

Stewart House
24 Kingsway
London WC2B 6JX
Tel: 0171-664 7208

Crossroads Care Attendant Schemes
Volunteers to help care for your
relative at home

10 Regent Place
Rugby
Warwickshire CV21 2PN
Tel: 01788 573653

CRUSE – Bereavement Care
Bereavement advice and support

126 Sheen Road
Richmond
Surrey TW9 1UR
Tel: 0181-940 4818

DIAL (Disablement Information
and Advice Lines)
Information and advice for people
with disabilities

Park Lodge
St Catherine's Hospital
Tickhill Road
Balby
Doncaster DN4 8QN
Tel: 01302 310123

Dial-A-Ride (DART)
Information about local dial-a-ride
and taxicard schemes

Unit 11
Spectrum House
32–34 Gordon House Road
London NW5 1LP
Tel: 0171-482 2325

Disability Alliance
Information on welfare benefits

1st Floor East
Universal House
88–94 Wentworth Street
London E1 7SA
Tel: 0171-247 8763

Disabled Living Foundation
Information about aids to help you
cope with a disability

380–384 Harrow Road
London W9 2HU
Tel: 0171-289 6111

121

DVLC (Driver Vehicle Licensing Centre)
Information on eligibility to drive

Customer Enquiry Unit
DVLC
Swansea SA6 7JL
Tel: 01792 772151

Energy Saving Trust
Advice line about saving household energy

Freephone: 0800 512012

Friends of Carers
Support for carers from individuals and companies

20–25 Glasshouse Yard
London EC1A 4JS
Tel: 0171-490 8818

Health Education Authority
Advice on general health issues

Hamilton House
Mabledon Place
London WC1H 9TX
Tel: 0171-383 3833

Help the Aged
Advice and support for older people and carers

16–18 St James' Walk
London EC1R 0BE
Tel: 0171-253 0253

Help the Aged Retirement Property Service (HARPS)
Free advice to buyers and sellers of retirement property nationwide

Freephone: 0800 592 605

Holiday Care Service
Information and advice about holidays for older or disabled people and carers

2nd Floor
Imperial Buildings
Victoria Road
Horley
Surrey RH6 7PZ
Tel: 01293 774535

Holidays for You and Me
Cottages adapted for people with disabilities

Caerau Bach
Croesgoch
Haverford West
Pembrokeshire SA62 5JU
Tel: 01348 837833

Home Energy Efficiency Scheme
Advice on savings in the home

Freephone: 0800 181 667
Minicom: 0191-233 1054

Incontinence Information Helpline
Advice for people with continence problems

Tel: 0191-213 0050
Monday to Friday
9am–6pm

John Grooms Association
Holiday accommodation for disabled people and carers

50 Scrutton Street
London EC2A 4PH
Tel: 0171-452 2000

Joseph Rowntree Foundation
Funds research into social problems; produces information, including advice about care of pets for older or disabled people

The Homestead
40 Water End
York YO3 6LP
Tel: 01904 629241

Local authority
Information on local government departments, social services, grants available

Look in the phone book under the name of your county, district, metropolitan or borough council, or Yellow Pages under 'Local Government'

MAVIS (Mobility Advice and Vehicle Information Service)
Advice on car adaptations and transport for disabled people

Department of Transport
Transport Research
  Laboratory
Old Wokingham Road
Crowthorne
Berkshire RG45 6AU
Tel: 01344 661000

MIND
Advice and support for people with mental illness and their families

Granta House
15–19 Broadway
London E15 4BQ
Tel: 0181-519 2122

National Debtline
Advice on financial difficulties

Tel: 0121-359 8501

National Council for Voluntary Organisations (NCVO)
Information on local voluntary organisations who may be able to provide help

Regents Wharf
8 All Saints Street
London N1 9RL
Tel: 0171-713 6161

New Ways to Work
Advice on flexible work arrangements

309 Upper Street
London N1 2TY
Tel: 0171-226 4026

Office of Care and Protection
Information on power of attorney
in Northern Ireland

Royal Courts of Justice
PO Box 410
Chichester Street
Belfast BT1 3JF

Public Trust Office
Advice on power of attorney

Stewart House
24 Kingsway
London WC2B 6JX
Tel: 0171-664 7208/7300

RADAR (Royal Association for
Disability and Rehabilitation)
Information about aids and mobility,
holidays and leisure

12 City Forum
250 City Road
London EC1V 8AF
Tel: 0171-250 3222

Relatives Association
Advice for relatives and friends
of people in care homes

5 Tavistock Place
London WC1 9SS
Tel: 0171-916 6055/
0181-201 9153

Relaxation for Living Trust
Telephone support line

Foxhill
30 Victoria Avenue
Shanklin
Isle of Wight PO37 6LS
Tel: 01983 868166

RNIB (Royal National Institute
for the Blind)
Advice and support for people
with sight difficulties

224 Great Portland Street
London W1N 6AA
Tel: 0171-388 1266

RNID (Royal National Institute
for Deaf People)
Advice and support for people
with hearing difficulties

19–23 Featherstone Street
London EC1Y 8SL
Tel: 0171-296 8000

RoSPA (Royal Society for the
Prevention of Accidents)
Information leaflets

Edgbaston Park
353 Bristol Road
Birmingham B5 7ST
Tel: 0121-248 2000

Samaritans
Someone to talk to if you are
in despair

See your local directory

Saneline
Helpline for people with mental
illness or their families

Tel: 0345 678000
(2pm–midnight)

Social services

Address in local
telephone directory

Standing Conference of Ethnic
Minority Senior Citizens
Support and advice for older people
from ethnic minorities and their
families

5 Westminster Bridge Road
London SE1 7XW
Tel: 0171-928 0095

Talking Pages
Free information about services
(a 'talking' Yellow Pages)

Freephone: 0800 600 800

Tripscope
Information about travel in London
and the southwest

The Courtyard
Evelyn Road
London W4 5JL
Tel: 0345 585641

TUC (Trades Union Congress)
Advice on trade union matters

Congress House
Great Russell Street
London WC1B 3LS
Tel: 0171-636 4030

UKHCA (United Kingdom Homecare
Association)
Information on member organisations

42 Banstead Road
Carshalton Beeches
Surrey SM5 3NW
Helpline: 0181-288 1551

Winged Fellowship
Holidays for disabled people

Angel House
20–32 Pentonville Road
London N1 9XD
Tel: 0171-833 2594

125

Winter Warmth Line
Information and advice
(October–March)

Freephone: 0800 289404
Northern Ireland:
0800 616757
Scotland:
0800 838587

War Pensioners' Welfare Service
Advice about state benefits

See local telephone directory

WRVS (Women's Royal Voluntary Service)
Often provides meals-on-wheels

Address in local telephone directory

About Age Concern

Caring for someone at a distance is one of a wide range of publications produced by Age Concern England, the National Council on Ageing. Age Concern cares about all older people and believes later life should be fulfilling and enjoyable. For too many this is impossible. As the leading charitable movement in the UK concerned with ageing and older people, Age Concern finds effective ways to change that situation.

Where possible, we enable older people to solve problems themselves, providing as much or as little support as they need. Our network of 1,400 local groups, supported by 250,000 volunteers, provides community-based services such as lunch clubs, day centres and home visiting.

Nationally, we take a lead role campaigning, parliamentary work, policy analysis, research, specialist information and advice provision, and publishing. Innovative programmes promote healthier lifestyles and provide older people with opportunities to give the experience of a lifetime back to their communities.

Age Concern is dependent on donations, covenants and legacies.

Age Concern England
1268 London Road
London SW16 4ER
Tel: 0181-679 8000

Age Concern Cymru
4th Floor
1 Cathedral Road
Cardiff CF1 9SD
Tel: 01222 371566

Age Concern Scotland
113 Rose Street
Edinburgh EH2 3DT
Tel: 0131-220 3345

Age Concern Northern Ireland
3 Lower Crescent
Belfast BT7 1NR
Tel: 01232 245729

127

Other books in this series

The Carer's Handbook: What to do and who to turn to
Marina Lewycka
At some point in their lives millions of people find themselves suddenly responsible for organising the care of an older person with a health crisis. All too often such carers have no idea what services are available or who can be approached for support. This book is designed to act as a first point of reference in just such an emergency, signposting readers to many more detailed, local sources of advice.
£6.99 0–86242–262–0

Caring for someone who is dying
Penny Mares
Confronting the knowledge that a loved one is going to die soon is always a moment of crisis. And the pain of the news can be compounded by the need to take responsibility for the care and support given in the last months and weeks. This book attempts to help readers cope with their emotions, identify the needs that the situation creates and make the practical arrangements necessary to ensure that passage through the period is as smooth as possible.
£6.99 0–86242–260–4

Finding and paying for residential and nursing home care
Marina Lewycka
Acknowledging that an older person needs residential care often represents a major crisis for family and friends. Feelings of guilt and betrayal invariably compound the difficulties faced in identifying a suitable care home and sorting out the financial arrangements. This book provides a practical step-by-step guide to the decisions that have to be made and the help that is available.
£6.99 0–86242–261–2

Choices for the carer of an older relative
Marina Lewycka
Being a carer may mean many different things – from living at a distance and keeping a check on things by telephone to taking on a full-time caring role. This book looks at the choices facing someone whose parent or other relative needs care. It helps readers look at their own circumstances and their own priorities and decide what is the best role for themselves – as well as the person being cared for.
£6.99 0–86242–263–9

Caring for someone who has dementia
Jane Brotchie
Caring for someone with dementia can be physically and emotionally exhausting, and it is often difficult to think about what can be done to make the situation easier. This book shows how to cope and seek further help as well as containing detailed information on the illness itself and what to expect in the future.
£6.99 0–86242–259–0

Caring for someone who has had a stroke
Philip Coyne and Penny Mares
Although 100,000 people in Britain will have a stroke this year, many people are still confused about what stroke actually means. This books is designed to help carers understand stroke and its immediate aftermath. It contains extensive information on hospital discharge, providing care, rehabilitation, and adjustment to life at home.
£6.99 0–86242–264–7

Caring for someone with an alcohol problem
Mike Ward
£6.99 0-86242-227-2

Publications from Age Concern Books

Money matters

Your Rights: A guide to money benefits for older people
Sally West

A highly acclaimed annual guide to the state benefits available to older people. Contains current information on Income Support, Housing Benefit and Retirement Pensions, among other matters, and provides advice on how to claim.

For further information, please telephone 0181-679 8000

Managing Other People's Money (2nd edition)
Penny Letts

Foreword by the Master of the Court of Protection

The management of money and property is usually a personal and private matter. However, there may come a time when someone else has to take over on either a temporary or a permanent basis. This book looks at the circumstances in which such a need could arise and provides a step-by-step guide to the arrangements that have to be made.

£9.99 0–86242–250–7

Ethnic Elders' Benefits Handbook
Sue Ward

Written in clear and concise English, this book aims to help anyone from an ethnic minority understand how the Social Security benefits system works, what their rights are and how they can claim a benefit to which they may be entitled. It includes explanations of the legal issues covering immigration and citizenship.

£9.99 0–86242–229–9

Health and care

The Community Care Handbook: The reformed system explained (2nd edition)

Barbara Meredith

The delivery of care in the community has changed dramatically as a result of recent legislation, and continues to evolve. Written by one of the country's foremost experts, this book explains in practical terms the background to the reforms, what they are, how they operate and whom they affect.

£13.99 0–86242–171–3

Know Your Medicines (3rd edition)

Pat Blair

This popular guide covers, in clear language, many of the common questions that older people – and those who care for them – may have about the medicines they use and how these may affect them.

£7.99 0–86242–226–4

If you would like to order any of these titles, please write to the address below, enclosing a cheque or money order for the appropriate amount made payable to Age Concern England. Credit card orders may be made on 0181-679 8000.

Mail Order Unit
Age Concern England
1268 London Road
London SW16 4ER

Factsheets from Age Concern

Covering many areas of concern to older people, Age Concern's factsheets are comprehensive and totally up to date. There are over 40 factsheets, with each one providing straightforward information and impartial advice in a simple and easy-to-use format. Topics covered include:

- finding and paying for residential and nursing home care
- raising income from your home
- money benefits
- legal arrangements for managing financial affairs
- finding help at home

Single copies are available free on receipt of a 9" × 12" sae.

Age Concern offers a factsheet subscription service which presents all the factsheets in a folder, together with regular updates throughout the year. The first year's subscription currently costs £40; an annual renewal thereafter is £20.

For further information, or to order factsheets, write to:

Information and Policy Division
Age Concern England
1268 London Road
London SW16 4ER

For readers in Scotland wishing further information, or to order factsheets, please write to:

Age Concern Scotland
113 Rose Street
Edinburgh EH2 3DT

Subscribers in Scotland will be automatically sent Scottish editions of factsheets where law and practice differ in Scotland.

Index